South African COOKING IN THE USA

AILEEN WILSEN

KATHLEEN FARQUHARSON

South African Cooking in the USA

Copyright © 2010, 2015
Aileen Wilsen and Kathleen Farquharson

Perfectbound ISBN: 978-1-62654-203-7
Spiralbound ISBN: 978-1-62654-218-1

Published by Echo Point Books & Media
Brattleboro, Vermont
www.EchoPointBooks.com

Interior Layout and Cover Design: Rachel Boothby Gualco
Editorial and Proofreading Assistance: Ian Straus

PRINTED IN THE UNITED STATES OF AMERICA

In loving memory of Hannes Watermeyer,
our father and Oupie.

Table of Contents

Preface

South African cuisine is a unique fusion of African, European and Eastern cooking styles and flavors, with strong influences from the Netherlands, Indonesia, France, Germany, Britain, India and Portugal.

This collection of recipes contains many traditional and contemporary South African favorites, adjusted for easy preparation in the USA. It includes tips on obtaining hard-to-find ingredients and offers a variety of readily available substitutes.

Our sincerest thanks to those who assisted with this project, supporting us with recipes, suggestions and encouragement. Annatjie Carstens shared a handwritten collection of recipes that is not only a wonderful record of tradition, but also a work of art. A special word of thanks to Noleen du Toit, Joan Duminy, Anita Fourie and Lies Rabinowitz for their generous and enthusiastic contributions. Thank you also to Debs Fisher, Colleen and Erica Watermeyer, Gordon and Margaret Farquharson, Milly Kulenkampff, Heide Rossouw, and Brown, Craig, Erika and John Wilsen.

We hope you enjoy creating South African dishes in your own kitchen, and that some of these dishes will become favorites in your household.

Aileen and Kathy
May 31, 2010

Notes on Ingredients

Amarula – cream-based liqueur made from the fruit of the marula tree (also known as the elephant tree, as elephants are fond of its fruit). Similar to Bailey's Irish Cream. Imported from South Africa and found in many local liquor stores.

brown sugar – either dark brown or crunchy brown sugar.

butter – sweet butter, either salted or unsalted.

butter/cream cheese, room temperature – remove from the refrigerator 30 minutes before use.

chutney – a spicy, fruity condiment frequently served as an accompaniment to meats. Frequently stocked in the international food aisle and in international food markets and stores.

cinnamon-sugar – ½ teaspoon ground cinnamon mixed with ¼ cup white sugar.

crunchy brown sugar – dry, granulated brown sugar.

curry powder – Indian-style blend of spices (mild or hot), typically yellow/orange in color due to the presence of turmeric and chili. Available in the spice section of most supermarkets. Imported South African curry powder (e.g., Raja and Cartwright curry powder) is usually stocked in South African specialty stores.

custard powder – cornstarch-based powder that is mixed with milk to make custard. Available in the international aisle of some supermarkets, or in specialty British and South African food stores.

dark brown sugar – fine, moist/packed brown sugar.

eggs – large.

flour – all-purpose white flour, unless otherwise stipulated.

golden syrup – refined cane sugar with a viscous consistency. Often available in the international aisle of supermarkets, in delis, and in British and South African specialty food stores. When used as an accompaniment, golden syrup can be substituted with honey, maple syrup or agave nectar.

guavas – pale pink tropical fruit with a distinctive flavor and hard, edible pips in the center. Fresh or canned guavas are not widely available in local supermarkets. Guava paste and guava nectar are sometimes stocked in the Spanish section of supermarkets. Canned guava halves in heavy syrup are often sold in South African specialty food stores. Guava juice or nectar can sometimes be found in the international aisle of supermarkets, and guava juice is frequently stocked in South African specialty stores.

Marmite – salty yeast extract generally used as a spread for sandwiches or toast. Available in the international section of some supermarkets or at specialty British or South African food stores.

oil – vegetable oil, such as canola or sunflower, unless otherwise stipulated.

shredded coconut, unsweetened – dried coconut. The unsweetened variety is sold in natural food stores.

sugar – granulated white cane sugar, unless otherwise stipulated.

Tennis biscuits – square cookies that are similar to Maria biscuits, but contain finely shredded coconut. They are sold in South African specialty stores.

Measurements

The recipes in this book were tested using standard USA measuring cups and spoons. Temperature is given in degrees Fahrenheit (°F).

General conversions

US measuring unit	US fluid measurement equivalent	US cup equivalent	Metric equivalent (approximate)
1 teaspoon			4.93 ml (5 ml)
1 tablespoon (3 teaspoons)			14.79 ml (15 ml)
2 tablespoons	1 ounce		29.57 ml (30 ml)
4 tablespoons	2 ounces	¼ cup	59.15 ml (60 ml)
8 tablespoons	4 ounces	½ cup	118.29 ml (125 ml)
16 tablespoons	8 ounces	1 cup	236.59 ml (250 ml)
1 pint	16 ounces	2 cups	473.18 ml (½ l)
1 quart	2 pints	4 cups	946.35 ml (1 l)
1 gallon	4 quarts	16 cups	3.79 l
Mass/weight (on scale)			
1 pound	16 ounces		0.454 kg

US measuring unit			Metric equivalent (approximate)
Dimensions (e.g., diameters of cake tins)			
1 inch			2.54 cm
7 inches			18 cm
8 inches			20 cm
9 inches			23 cm
10 inches			25 cm
11 inches			28 cm
12 inches			30 cm
Oven temperatures			
200°F			100°C
250°F			120°C
300°F			150°C
325°F			160°C
350°F			180°C
375°F			190°C
400°F			200°C
425°F			220°C

Note of Caution: Undercooked eggs, meat, fish and poultry may contain bacteria that cause disease. For recipes in which the egg may not get adequately heated, egg substitute can be used as a precaution. The recipes have been carefully tested, but results will vary depending on the ingredients, altitude and oven temperature.

Terminology

In South Africa...	In the USA...
bicarbonate of soda	baking soda
biscuit	cookie
braai	barbecue
braaivleis	barbecued meat
bredie	stew
bringal, aubergine	eggplant
cornflour, Maizena	cornstarch
courgette, baby marrow	zucchini
crumpet, flapjack	pancake
crushed garlic	minced garlic
desiccated coconut	shredded coconut
dhania (coriander) leaves	cilantro
gherkin	pickle
grated cheese	shredded cheese
icing sugar	confectioners powder sugar
icing	frosting
ideal milk	evaporated milk
jam	preserves, jelly
jam roll, Swiss roll	jelly roll
jelly	jello
mielie	corn
mieliemeal	cornmeal
mince or minced meat	ground meat
oreganum	oregano
pancake	large crêpe
pickling onions	boiler onions
plait	braid
rashers of bacon	strips of bacon
self-raising flour	self-rising flour
soya sauce	soy sauce
spanspek, sweet melon	cantaloupe
spring onion	green onion
sweets	candy
tomato sauce	ketchup

Kaapse vetkoek Souttert

Bunny chow

Mulligatawny

Cold lemon soup

Snacks, Starters & Light Meals

Worsrolletjies

Cocktail sausage rolls.

Yield: 28-36

1 tablespoon oil
1 onion, finely chopped
½ pound ground pork
2 cloves garlic, crushed
¾ teaspoon dried thyme
½ teaspoon salt
dash of black pepper

2 sheets frozen puff pastry

1. Heat the oil in a small pan and sauté the onion for a few minutes.
2. Add the remaining ingredients and stir over medium-high heat until the meat is lightly browned and cooked.
3. Chill well.
4. Thaw the pastry as per directions on the package. Unfold, roll lightly and cut each sheet into two rectangular strips.
5. Divide the cold ground meat between the pastry strips and arrange it lengthwise down the center of each strip.
6. Wet the long edges of the pastry with cold water and fold over to form four long sausages. Crimp the edge lightly and cut into 1–1½ inch pieces with a sharp knife.
7. Arrange on a lined or lightly greased baking tray and bake at 400° F for 10–15 minutes, until the pastry is puffed up and golden.

Chili bites

Yield: 24-30

1 cup flour
1 ½ teaspoons baking powder
1 small onion, finely chopped
2 green chilies, seeded and diced
½ cup cilantro leaves, chopped
1 teaspoon ground cumin
½ teaspoon hot chili powder
¾ teaspoon salt
½ cup water, approximately

oil for frying

1. Mix the flour, baking powder, onion, chilies, cilantro, cumin, chili powder and salt in a bowl.
2. Add water to form a dropping batter.
3. Pour oil into a heavy-based saucepan, to a depth of about an inch, and heat.
4. Drop small spoonfuls of the batter into the oil and fry until lightly browned on all sides.
5. Drain on paper toweling.
6. Skewer with toothpicks and serve hot or at room temperature with Chutney dip (page 22).

Samoosas

Pastry triangles with a spicy, crumbly, filling. Originally from Persia, variations of these tasty treats are found worldwide. Samoosas arrived in South Africa via Indian immigrants, were adopted by the Cape Malay community and became an integral part of South African cuisine.

Yield: 4-5 dozen

Meat filling
1 tablespoon oil
1 pound ground beef or lamb
¾ teaspoon salt
1½ teaspoons ground cumin
½ teaspoon turmeric
1 teaspoon chili powder
2 cloves garlic, crushed
1 teaspoon grated fresh ginger root
½ cup cilantro leaves, chopped
2 medium onions, finely chopped

18-20 egg roll wrappers
2-3 cups oil for deep frying

1. Heat 1 tablespoon of oil in a pan and brown the meat until crumbly.
2. Add the salt, cumin, turmeric, chili powder, garlic and ginger. Mix well and simmer for 10 minutes.
3. Mix in the cilantro and onion. Stir over medium heat for about 5 minutes and set aside to cool.
4. Fold each egg roll wrapper into thirds (approximately 2¼ x 7 inches), unfold, and cut along the folds to give three separate strips.
5. Taking one strip at a time, fold the lower edge over to the right, to form a triangle (see diagram).

6. Fold the pastry upwards across the top of the triangle.
7. Rotate the open side of the triangle to the left to form a pocket in which to place the filling. The strip is now above the opening.
8. Pick up the pastry strip and fill the pocket with 1-2 teaspoons of the filling.
9. Fold the pastry across the top of the pouch to seal the opening.
10. Wet the remaining straight edges of the strip with cold water and fold them neatly around the triangle.
11. Pinch the corners lightly to seal and puff the pouch.
12. Set the folded samoosas aside on a platter until all the filling has been used. Lightly cover the folded samoosas and the egg roll sheets with a damp dishcloth or paper toweling, so that they do not dry out.
13. Deep-fry the samoosas in oil, a few at a time, over medium heat. If the oil is too hot, the pastry will blister.
14. Turn the samoosas over to cook evenly.
15. When golden brown on both sides, remove from the oil and drain on paper toweling.

Notes

Pur, the pastry used for samoosas, is very time consuming to make. Although not authentic, phyllo pastry can be used instead of pur. Traditionally, strips of approximately 2 x 10 inches are used. Egg roll wrappers may be closer to the genuine product, but their dimensions make them a little awkward to fold.

The filling must be cold, dry and crumbly when the samoosas are made, to prevent the pastry from softening and losing shape.

For bite-sized samoosas, egg roll wrappers can be cut into 4 strips of pastry. About ½ teaspoon of filling is used per pouch and there are more layers of pastry surrounding the triangle.

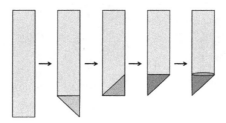

Chicken liver paté

Yield: 1¼ cups

1 pound chicken livers
3 tablespoons butter
1 small onion, chopped
1 clove garlic, crushed
1 teaspoon dried thyme
1 tablespoon lemon juice
1 teaspoon Worcestershire sauce
3 tablespoons cream
2½ tablespoons sherry
salt and pepper

4 tablespoons (½ stick) butter

1. Use kitchen shears to cut away any hard bits in the liver.
2. Melt 3 tablespoons of butter in a pan and sauté the liver, onion and garlic until the liver is cooked. Set aside to cool.
3. Liquidize or blend all the ingredients, except the 4 tablespoons of butter, until smooth and creamy. Adjust the consistency with a tablespoon or two of boiling water.
4. Season to taste and scoop the pâté into ramekins or an earthenware crock.
5. Melt the 4 tablespoons of butter and pour over the surface of the pâté to prevent discoloration.
6. Cover and refrigerate for at least a day before serving so that the flavors can blend and mellow.
7. Serve with fresh brown bread (page 182).

Mock smoked snoek pâté

Cape snoek (Thyrsites atun) *is an oily fish with a distinctive flavor, native to South African waters.*

Yield: 1 ½ cups

2 3.25-ounce cans kipper snacks, drained
1 small onion, finely chopped
½ cup regular cream cheese
2 tablespoons sour cream
2 tablespoons lemon juice
¼ teaspoon salt

1. Blend or mix all the ingredients together.
2. Adjust the flavoring and scoop into an earthenware crock or ramekin.
3. Cover and chill for at least a few hours before serving with fresh brown bread (page 182), Melba toast or crackers.

Notes
Kipper snacks (i.e., smoked herring) make a good substitute for smoked snoek in this recipe.

Chutney dip

Yield: 2 cups

1 cup whipped cream cheese
½ cup sour cream
1 teaspoon crushed garlic
1 teaspoon finely chopped onion
½ cup fruit chutney (page 10, page 192)
¼ teaspoon cayenne pepper
paprika

1. Blend together all the ingredients, except the paprika.
2. Scoop into an attractive bowl and sprinkle with paprika.
3. Serve with a selection of chips, crackers, crudités
   (e.g., carrots, celery sticks, green onions, mushrooms,
   broccoli and cauliflower florets, cucumber, radishes, cherry
   tomatoes) spicy kebaabs (page 25) or chili bites (page 17).

Peppadew dip

A peppery party dip.

Yield: 2 cups

1 cup regular cream cheese
½ cup sour cream
8 green onions, finely chopped
2 cloves garlic, crushed
1 cup drained and chopped peppadews

1. Blend or mix all the ingredients together.
2. Scoop the mixture into an attractive bowl or ramekin.
3. Cover and chill for at least a couple of hours before serving with chips, crackers, Melba toast or crudités (e.g., carrots, celery sticks, green onions, mushrooms, broccoli and cauliflower florets, cucumber, radishes, cherry tomatoes).

Notes

Jars of imported peppadews (peppery fruits reminiscent of miniature red peppers) are available in the preserved vegetable section of some specialty supermarkets.

A whole peppadew or peppadew rings make an attractive garnish.

Devils on horseback

Tasty little morsels for the hors d'oeuvres platter.

stoned prunes and/or dates
salted almonds
chutney (page 10, page 192)
hot mustard
slices of bacon

toothpicks

1. Fill the prune and date cavities with a salted almond and/or a little chutney.
2. Spread a layer of mustard onto each slice of bacon and cut the bacon in half widthwise.
3. Wrap dates and prunes in bacon.
4. Arrange on a baking sheet, seam side down.
5. Broil for a few minutes, or bake at 350° F for 15-20 minutes, until crisp and lightly browned. Turn to brown evenly.
6. Skewer with a toothpick and arrange on a platter. Serve hot.

Notes

Angels on horseback are similar, but consist of oysters wrapped in bacon, without mustard. Use canned oysters, or marinate fresh oysters in dry white wine and crushed garlic.
Bake or broil as above.

Spicy kebaabs

Deep-fried cocktail meatballs.

Yield: 24-30

1 pound ground beef
3 cloves garlic, crushed
1 teaspoon grated fresh ginger root
1 small onion, finely chopped
¾ teaspoon salt
¼ teaspoon cayenne pepper
1 teaspoon chili powder
1 teaspoon ground cumin
1 egg, whisked

1-2 cups oil for deep-frying

1. Mix the beef, garlic, ginger, onion, salt, pepper, chili powder, cumin and egg together in a mixing bowl until blended.
2. Shape into small balls and deep-fry in heated oil until golden brown and cooked through.
3. Drain on paper toweling.
4. Skewer with toothpicks and serve with Chutney dip (page 22).

Notes
Instead of frying the kebaabs, they can be placed in a greased, ovenproof dish and baked in the oven at 350° F for 20-30 minutes.

Devilled eggs

Stuffed hard-boiled eggs.

Yield: 10

5 eggs
2 tablespoons mayonnaise
2 tablespoons cream
¼ teaspoon salt
½ teaspoon ground mustard
black pepper
1 tablespoon finely chopped parsley
sprigs of parsley

1. Place the eggs in a pot of cold water and bring to the boil. Boil for 10 minutes, drain and crack the shells under cold running water. Shell the eggs when cold.
2. Cut each egg in half and carefully remove the yolk.
3. Mash or blend the yolks with the remaining ingredients. Adjust the flavoring to taste.
4. Fill egg white halves with the yolk mixture using two spoons or a piping bag, and garnish with sprigs of parsley. If necessary, cut a sliver of egg white from the base to stabilize the halves on a serving platter.

Spanspek with Parma ham

Cantaloupe with prosciutto.

Legend has it that "Spanspek" (literally "Spanish bacon") got its name because Lady Juana (1798-1872), the Spanish wife of Governor Harry Smith, preferred cantaloupe to bacon for breakfast.

1 cantaloupe or sweet melon, peeled, seeded and cut into bite-sized chunks
prosciutto, cut into strips
toothpicks

1. Wrap pieces of prosciutto around cantaloupe chunks and secure with toothpicks.
2. Serve chilled on a platter with mixed hors d'oeuvres.

Notes
Pears can be used instead of cantaloupe in this recipe.

Cheese puffs

Savory, scone-like snacks.

Yield: 20 small puffs

1 ½ cups flour
2 teaspoons baking powder
¼ teaspoon salt
1 cup grated sharp Cheddar cheese
½ teaspoon ground mustard
¼ teaspoon cayenne or black pepper
1 cup milk

1. Mix all the ingredients in a mixing bowl, cutting in the milk lightly.
2. Spoon the batter into small, shallow muffin pans and bake at 375° F for 10–15 minutes. Serve as is, or with butter.

Notes

For extra flavor and a bit of color, mix in 1 tablespoon of chopped chives and/or 2 rashers of cooked and crumbled bacon.

Cheese straws

Yield: 24-26

1 sheet frozen puff pastry, thawed
prepared mustard, optional
finely grated Parmesan cheese
garlic salt
cayenne pepper

1. Unfold the pastry and roll out lightly to about half the original thickness, on a lightly floured surface.
2. Spread a thin layer of mustard over half the pastry (optional step) and sprinkle with cheese, salt and pepper to taste.
3. Fold the other half of the pastry over the cheese layer and press together lightly.
4. Cut lengthwise into ¼-inch wide strips.
5. Cut each strip in half.
6. Lift each straw carefully and twist firmly to form a tight spiral.
7. Arrange on a lined baking tray.
8. Bake at 400° F for 8-12 minutes, until puffed up and lightly browned.

Notes

Finely crushed fresh garlic and plain salt can be used instead of garlic salt.

Souttert

Savory tart.

4-6 servings

2 eggs
½ pound lean bacon or ham, cut into small pieces
1 medium onion, finely chopped
½ tablespoon oil, optional
3 tablespoons flour
1 teaspoon prepared mustard
2 tablespoons dried parsley
2 cups grated sharp cheese (e.g., Cheddar, Gruyère)

4 eggs
1 ½ cups milk
½ teaspoon salt
dash of black or cayenne pepper

1. Place 2 eggs in a saucepan and cover with cold water. Heat to boiling point and boil for 10 minutes. Remove from stove and crack the shells under cold, running water. Shell and chop the eggs coarsely when cool. Set aside.
2. Sauté the bacon and onion in a small frying pan until the bacon is cooked. Add a little oil if necessary. If using ham, sauté the onion until glassy and add the ham.
3. Sprinkle the flour over the bacon/ham and onion. Mix.
4. Add the chopped eggs, mustard, parsley and cheese. Mix well and spoon into a deep, greased 9-inch pie dish.
5. Whisk the remaining eggs, milk, salt and pepper in a jug and pour over the mixture.
6. Bake at 350° F for 50-60 minutes, until set and lightly browned.

Tuna pizza

Easy, yeast-free pizza base.

4-6 servings

Base
1 cup flour
1 ½ teaspoons baking powder
¼ teaspoon salt
2 ½ tablespoons oil
⅓ cup milk

Topping
3-4 cups grated sharp cheese, e.g., Cheddar
2 large tomatoes, diced
1 5-ounce can tuna in water or oil, drained and coarsely shredded
2 teaspoons dried thyme
1 medium onion, chopped
1 medium green pepper, seeded and diced
pitted black olives

1. Sift the flour, baking powder and salt into a bowl and cut in the oil and milk.
2. Knead the dough until elastic. Press the dough into a 10-inch pizza pan or platter to form a thin layer. This will require careful pressing and stretching. Prick the base with a fork and set it aside for at least 30 minutes before baking.
3. Cover the base, right up to the edge, with the cheese.
4. Top with the remaining ingredients.
5. Bake at 400° F for 10 minutes and then reduce the oven temperature to 350° F for a further 15 to 20 minutes.

Spinach roulade

Savory spinach roll filled with creamy mushroom sauce.

4-6 servings

Filling
4 tablespoons (½ stick) butter or margarine
6 ounces fresh mushrooms, thinly sliced
2 cloves garlic, crushed
3 tablespoons flour
¼ teaspoon salt
¼ teaspoon ground nutmeg
½ cup milk
¼ cup finely chopped chives or green onion

Base
½ pound frozen chopped spinach
1 tablespoon butter or margarine
1 tablespoon flour
4 eggs, separated
½ teaspoon salt
freshly ground black pepper

½ cup grated Parmesan cheese

1. Line a baking tray, approximately 9½ x 14 inches, with parchment paper. Set aside.
2. First make the filling. Melt the butter in a saucepan and fry the mushrooms with garlic until tender.
3. Lower the heat, sprinkle with flour, salt and nutmeg, and mix.
4. Add the milk, stirring constantly until the mixture thickens.
5. Mix in the chives, adjust the flavoring, cover with a lid and set aside.

6. Now make the base. Place the spinach in a microwave-safe dish with a lid and microwave on full power for 4-6 minutes, stirring once. Do not add any water. Drain out any excess liquid by pressing the spinach with the back of a large spoon.
7. Stir the butter into the hot spinach.
8. Add the flour, egg yolks and seasoning and mix well.
9. Beat the egg whites to the soft-peak stage and fold into the spinach mixture.
10. Spread out onto the parchment paper and sprinkle with the cheese.
11. Bake at 350° F for 10-12 minutes, until set.
12. Turn the base out onto a damp dishcloth and carefully peel off the parchment paper.
13. Spread the mushroom filling over the base, leaving a ½-inch margin on both long and one of the short sides.
14. Starting from the short side that has filling all the way to the edge, roll up carefully to form a neat roll. Lift the dishcloth to facilitate the rolling process.
15. Leave dishcloth around the roulade for 10-20 minutes.
16. Transfer to an attractive serving platter, seam side down. Serve warm.

Notes
The roulade can be made ahead of time and reheated. Cover lightly with foil, shiny side down, and place in the oven at 300° F for 20-30 minutes.

Crustless zucchini and corn quiche

4-6 servings

2 tablespoons (¼ stick) butter
1 medium onion, chopped
1½ pounds zucchini, sliced
1 large clove garlic, crushed
1 14.75-ounce can cream style corn
½+1 cup grated sharp Cheddar cheese
¼ teaspoon salt
pepper
¾ teaspoon dried thyme
3 eggs, whisked

1. Melt the butter in a large frying pan.
2. Add the onion and zucchini and sauté until lightly browned. Remove from the heat.
3. Add the garlic, corn, ½ cup cheese and seasoning. Mix well.
4. Stir in the egg and pour into a greased, ovenproof dish.
5. Sprinkle the remaining cheese over the top and bake at 350° F for 40-50 minutes, until set.

Kaapse vetkoek

Rich, crispy "Cape fat cakes".

Yield: 12

2 cups flour
2 teaspoons baking powder
½ teaspoon salt
2 eggs
1 cup water

1-2 cups oil

1. Sift the dry ingredients into a mixing bowl.
2. Whisk the eggs with the water and cut into the dry ingredients to form a dropping batter.
3. Cover the base of a frying pan with oil and heat.
4. Drop large spoonfuls of the batter into the heated oil and fry on both sides until light brown and cooked through.
5. Drain on paper toweling, cut in half, horizontally, and fill with curried mince (page 73).

Notes
A yeast bread dough (e.g., white bread dough page 180), fried in oil after the second rising, can also be used to make vetkoek.

Vetkoek is also served with curried chicken (page 62), curried vegetables (page 111) or bacon and eggs. The meal can be rounded off with vetkoek decked with honey or golden syrup (page 11) and grated cheese.

Spinach pancakes

Substantial crêpes with a spinach and hard-boiled egg filling.

Yield: 8 pancakes

Pancakes
1 cup flour
pinch of salt
1 egg
¾ cup milk
¾ cup water
2 tablespoons oil

1 lb pre-washed baby spinach

Cheese sauce
2 tablespoons (¼ stick) butter or margarine
3 tablespoons flour
salt and pepper
milk, made up to 1 cup with water drained from boiled spinach
1 cup grated sharp Cheddar cheese

4 eggs
paprika

1. Make the pancake batter by blending all the pancake ingredients together until smooth.
2. Cover and set aside for at least an hour before using.
3. Boil the spinach until wilted. Cut coarsely and drain over a bowl, squeezing out any excess water (retain for the cheese sauce).
4. Melt the butter in a saucepan and stir in the flour and seasoning.
5. Add the liquid and continue stirring over medium heat until the sauce is thick and smooth.
6. Add the spinach and cheese and mix well. Set aside.
7. Make the pancakes, greasing the pan for the first pancake only.
8. While preparing the pancakes, place 4 eggs in a pot of cold water and bring to the boil. Boil for 10 minutes. Crack the shells under cold, running water, shell and chop coarsely.
9. To assemble, place a pancake on a large plate. Cover half with a portion of the spinach sauce.
10. Top with coarsely chopped or sliced egg and fold the pancake in half.
11. Garnish with a sprinkling of paprika.

Notes

Pancake batter can be made the day before. Cover and refrigerate until needed.

Bunny chow

There are many stories about the origin of this name, most of which link it to the banias, Hindu merchants and traders from India. In the mid-1800s, many Indians moved to what was then the British colony of Natal to work on the sugar plantations. From this group, the traders or banias emerged.

The banias saw the need for take-out food before the age of Styrofoam and plastic, and found that hollowed out loaves of bread made suitable containers. Thus, bread filled with curries became known as "bania chow" ("chow" is slang for "food"), which evolved into "bunny chow". Buns or vetkoek (page 35) filled with curry became known as "curry bunnies".

2 servings

1 loaf white bread, unsliced
curried mince, page 73 or
hot Durban curry, page 69 or
curried vegetables, page 111

1. Cut the bread transversally (i.e., halfway between the ends) and prop up the halves on their bases/heels.
2. Hollow out the soft center bread to form a bowl.
3. Fill each half with a generous serving of curry.
4. Cover with a lid of soft bread.

Notes
These servings are very large. For smaller portions, the loaf can be cut into 3 transverse sections, which would create one so-called "funny bunny", without a lower crust to contain the sauciness. This is rather awkward to eat.

Mulligatawny

Derived from the Tamil for "pepper water" or "pepper broth".
This soup became popular with British employees of the East
India Company during colonial times.

4 servings

2 tablespoons (¼ stick) butter or margarine
1 medium onion, diced
1 large carrot, diced
4 celery sticks, chopped
1 tablespoon flour
2 teaspoons curry powder
2 pints (4 cups) water
1 green cooking apple (e.g., Granny Smith), peeled and diced
½ cup cooked chicken, diced
½ cup cooked long grain rice
½ teaspoon salt
pepper

1. Melt the butter in a heavy-based saucepan, and sauté the onion, carrot and celery for 2-3 minutes.
2. Sprinkle the flour and curry powder over the vegetables and stir over medium heat until well mixed.
3. Stir in the water, cover with a lid and simmer for about 15 minutes.
4. Add the remaining ingredients, bring to the boil and simmer, covered, for 10-15 minutes.
5. Adjust flavoring and serve hot, with fresh brown bread (page 182).

Cold cucumber soup

4 servings

1 medium-sized English cucumber, unpeeled and coarsely grated
1 clove garlic, crushed
4 green onions, finely chopped
2 cups plain yogurt
¼ teaspoon salt

cream

1. Mix the cucumber, garlic, onion, yogurt and salt in a bowl.
2. Cover and refrigerate for at least three hours.
3. Scoop into attractive bowls and garnish with a swirl of cream.

Notes

For a richer, rounder soup, replace part of the yogurt with cream. For a smoother soup, liquidize the ingredients.

Cold lemon soup

An unusual, tangy soup, reminiscent of lemon meringue pie, served in the heat of summer.

4-6 servings

4 cups water
zest of 2 lemons
1 cup fresh lemon juice
¾ cup+3 tablespoons sugar
3 eggs, separated
¾ teaspoon vanilla extract
4½ tablespoons cornstarch
¼ cup cold water

1. Mix 4 cups of water, zest, lemon juice and ¾ cup of sugar in a saucepan.
2. Bring to the boil, while stirring.
3. Simmer for 10 minutes.
4. Whisk the vanilla into the yolks.
5. Mix the cornstarch with ¼ cup water and add to the yolks.
6. Slowly pour the hot lemon mixture over the yolks, stirring all the time.
7. Return to the saucepan and stir over medium heat until thick.
8. Chill well.
9. Before serving, beat the egg whites until frothy. Slowly add the remaining 3 tablespoons of sugar, and continue beating until stiff.
10. Float mounds of the sweet, white foam on top of the soup.

Notes

As a precaution, pasteurized eggs can be used.

Traditional bean soup

4-6 servings

1 ½ cups dried small red or Pinto beans
1 large onion, chopped
4-6 rashers bacon, cut into small pieces
2 carrots, cut into rounds
4 celery sticks, sliced
oil, optional
3 pints (6 cups) cold water
½ cup milk, optional
1 tablespoon lemon juice
salt and pepper

1. Rinse the beans and place them in a bowl with plenty of cold water. Soak overnight.
2. The next day, drain and rinse the beans.
3. In a heavy-based saucepan, sauté the onion, bacon, carrot and celery, over medium to high heat, for 2-3 minutes. Add a little oil if necessary.
4. Add the water and beans.
5. Boil for 1-2 hours, until the beans are soft.
6. Cool and mash, blend or liquidize about half of the soup and return it to the saucepan.
7. Adjust to desired consistency by adding a little water or milk.
8. Add the lemon juice and season to taste.
9. Serve with fresh brown bread (page 182) or dumplings (page 43).

Notes
Liquidize the whole batch for a smooth soup.

Smoked pork shank, hock or knuckle can be used instead of bacon. Add with the onion and vegetables.

Dumplings

10-12 dumplings

1 cup flour
1 ½ teaspoons baking powder
¼ teaspoon salt
1 tablespoon dried parsley
2 tablespoons (¼ stick) butter or margarine
⅔ cup water

1. Mix the flour, baking powder, salt and parsley in a bowl.
2. Rub the butter in lightly with the fingertips or a pastry cutter.
3. Mix in the water to form a soft, dropping dough. Do not overmix.
4. Drop spoonfuls on top of boiling soup or simmering stew/bredie.
5. Cover and simmer for 15–20 minutes.

Ham and pea soup

6–8 servings

1 cup dried split peas
1 tablespoon oil
1 smoked ham hock (shin)
2 large leeks, sliced
6–8 celery sticks, sliced
4 pints (8 cups) water
3 tablespoons lemon juice
salt and pepper

1. Rinse the peas under cold running water.
2. Heat the oil in a heavy-based saucepan, add the hock
    and vegetables and stir-fry over medium heat for
    5 minutes.
3. Add the peas and water and bring to the boil.
4. Reduce the heat, cover with a lid and leave to simmer for
    about 2 hours.
5. Remove the hock. Cut meaty bits off the bone, and add
    to the soup.
6. Cool slightly and blend until quite smooth.
7. Add the lemon juice and season to taste with salt and
    pepper.
8. Heat through and serve with dumplings (page 43) or
    fresh brown bread (page 182).

Cream of broccoli soup

4–6 servings

1 medium onion, coarsely chopped
1 tablespoon butter
1 medium potato, peeled and cubed
1 medium-large head of broccoli, washed and cut into pieces
2 pints (4 cups) vegetable or chicken stock
1 cup milk (approximately)
salt and pepper to taste

cream or plain yogurt

1. In a large saucepan, sauté the onion in the butter for a few minutes.
2. Add the potato and broccoli and stir over medium heat for about 5 minutes.
3. Add the stock, stir, and bring to the boil.
4. Cover with a lid and simmer for about 30 minutes, until the vegetables are soft.
5. Cool and liquidize or blend until smooth.
6. Add milk to achieve the desired consistency and adjust the flavoring.
7. Chill, if serving cold, or heat through before serving.
8. Garnish each serving with a swirl of cream or yogurt.

Mixed vegetable soup

6–8 servings

1 tablespoon oil
2 medium leeks, sliced
2 large carrots, sliced
1 large potato, diced
2 turnips, diced
1 bunch soup celery or table celery with leaves,
about 6 sticks
3 pints (6 cups) vegetable or chicken stock
½ cup dried soup mix
(or a mix of, for example, pearled barley, lentils, peas)
3 large tomatoes, skinned and diced
¼ teaspoon sugar
1 tablespoon lemon juice
salt and pepper

1. Heat the oil in a large saucepan and add the fresh
   vegetables, excluding the tomatoes. Stir-fry the
   vegetables over high heat for about 3 minutes.
2. Add the stock and bring to the boil.
3. Rinse the soup mix under cold, running water, and add
   to the soup. Stir, reduce heat, cover with a lid and
   simmer for an hour.
4. Add the tomatoes, sugar and lemon juice and simmer for
   a further 30 minutes.
5. Adjust the flavoring.

Notes
The soup can be partially or completely liquidized for a less
chunky or smooth soup.

Any mix of available vegetables can be used
(e.g., cabbage, butternut, broccoli, cauliflower, parsnip).

Soup is often tastier on the second day. Store, covered, in
the refrigerator and heat before serving.

This soup freezes well.

Melkkos met snysels

"Milk food with noodles"; comfort food for a cold winter's night. Traditionally, this was served to convalescents or as a light Sunday supper. More recently, it is served as a soup in student dining halls.

4 servings

Noodles
1 cup flour
pinch of salt
1 egg, whisked
water

Milk soup
4 cups milk
1 cinnamon stick
1 tablespoon butter

½ teaspoon ground cinnamon, mixed with
¼ cup sugar

1. First make the noodles. Combine the flour and salt in a bowl and mix in the egg with a fork.
2. Add a little water to form a stiff dough.
3. Knead until elastic and roll out very thinly on a lightly floured surface.
4. Leave to dry for about 20 minutes and then cut into thin strips.
5. Now make the soup. Bring the milk, with the cinnamon stick, to the boil in a medium-sized saucepan.
6. Add the noodles.
7. Simmer for about 30 minutes.
8. Stir in the butter.
9. Remove the cinnamon stick and ladle into bowls. Serve hot, sprinkled with cinnamon-sugar.

Mielieblompap

Cornstarch porridge; a variation of melkkos, made without the noodles.

4 servings

½ cup cornstarch
½+4 cups milk
1 cinnamon stick

½ teaspoon ground cinnamon, mixed with
¼ cup sugar

1. Combine the cornstarch with ½ cup cold milk in a bowl and mix to form a runny paste.
2. Heat the remaining 4 cups of milk, with the cinnamon stick, in a saucepan to just below boiling point.
3. Add some of the hot milk to the cornstarch and return to the saucepan, stirring constantly.
4. While continuing to stir, bring to the boil and simmer or 1-2 minutes, until thick and smooth.
5. Remove the cinnamon stick and serve, in bowls, with cinnamon-sugar.

Tomato bredie,

Monkeygland steak

Pickled fish

Oxtail stew Kedgeree

Chicken pie Frikkadelle

Mains

Fish breyani

A traditional Cape Malay entrée adapted from Indian cuisine.
This popular dish is served at special gatherings, such as
birthdays, weddings and funerals.

4-6 servings

1 tablespoon curry powder
1 tablespoon turmeric
3 cloves garlic, crushed
2 teaspoons grated fresh
ginger root
3 tablespoons oil
2 pounds firm white fish
(e.g., cod, halibut), filleted
and cut into portions

1½ cups rice

½ + ¼ teaspoon salt
½ teaspoon turmeric
3+1 cups water
½ cup dried lentils
oil for frying
2 onions, chopped
2-3 ripe tomatoes, skinned and
chopped
2 tablespoons chutney (page 10)
¼ teaspoon sugar
¼ teaspoon salt
1 tablespoon lemon juice
butter

1. Mix the curry, turmeric, garlic, ginger and oil to form a paste. Coat the fish and set aside for an hour.
2. Boil the rice, with ½ teaspoon salt and turmeric, in 3 cups of water, for 15 minutes. Drain.
3. Boil the lentils, with ¼ teaspoon salt, in 1 cup of water for 15 minutes. Drain.
4. Heat a little oil in a frying pan. Seal the fish on both sides in the hot oil. Remove the fish from the pan and set aside.
5. Fry the onion in the above frying pan, until glassy.
6. Add the tomato, chutney, sugar, salt and lemon juice, and simmer for 2 minutes.
7. Return the fish to the pan and mix.
8. In a casserole dish, layer half the rice, half the lentils and the fish mixture. Top with the remaining lentils, rice and tiny bits of butter.
9. Seal the dish with foil, covered with a lid, and bake at 300° F for 1 hour.

Pickled fish

Traditional curried fish.

6–8 servings

2 cups wine vinegar
2 cups water
6 bay leaves or lemon leaves
10 peppercorns
1 teaspoon salt
3 tablespoons flour
3 tablespoons mild curry powder
¼ cup smooth apricot jam

¼ cup dark brown sugar
3 pounds firm white fish (e.g., halibut), filleted and cut into portions
seasoned flour
oil and butter for frying
3 medium onions, sliced and broken into rings

1. Bring the vinegar, water, leaves, peppercorns and salt to the boil in a pan.
2. Mix the flour, curry powder, jam and sugar together. Add to the boiling vinegar mixture and simmer for about 10 minutes.
3. Meanwhile, lightly coat the fish with the seasoned flour.
4. Using half oil and half butter, fry the fish in a hot pan to seal it on both sides.
5. Reduce the heat and simmer until cooked through.
6. Add the onion to the simmering curry sauce and boil rapidly for 30 seconds.
7. Add the fish to the sauce, and simmer for 2 minutes.
8. Remove the fish, arrange in a glass dish, and top with the hot curry sauce.
9. Cover and chill for at least 24 hours before serving.

Fishcakes

Yield: 8-10

1 cup cooked fish, deboned and flaked
1 cup mashed potato
2 tablespoons dried parsley
1 tablespoon butter, room temperature
2 eggs, whisked and divided
salt
pinch of black or cayenne pepper
seasoned flour
dried breadcrumbs
oil for frying

1 lemon

1. Mix the fish, potato, parsley, butter and half the egg together in a mixing bowl.
2. Season to taste and divide into 8-10 patties.
3. Pour the remaining egg into a shallow bowl and sprinkle flour and breadcrumbs on separate sheets of wax wrap.
4. Coat the fish cakes with flour, then with egg and lastly with breadcrumbs.
5. Heat the oil in a frying pan and fry the fishcakes for 2-3 minutes, until golden brown.
6. Turn, and cook the other side until done.
7. Drain on paper toweling. Serve hot with lemon wedges and tartar sauce.

Tartar Sauce

Yield: 1 cup

½ cup mayonnaise
¼ cup sour cream
3 tablespoons finely chopped
pickle (gherkin)

2 teaspoons chopped capers
2 tablespoons finely chopped
or minced onion
paprika for garnish

1. Blend the ingredients together and refrigerate for at least a couple of hours.
2. Sprinkle with paprika and serve.

Notes

For a pale pink sauce, add a dash of paprika to the ingredients before blending.

Kedgeree

A rice-based fish dish.

4 servings

2 tablespoons (¼ stick) butter, melted
1 pound cooked fish
(e.g., haddock), deboned and coarsely flaked
¼ cup lemon juice

4 eggs, hard boiled, shelled and coarsely chopped
¼ cup finely chopped fresh parsley
3 cups cooked rice
salt and black pepper to taste
1 lemon, cut into wedges

1. Melt the butter in a large pan and add the fish and lemon juice.
2. Add the remaining ingredients, excluding the lemon, and mix.
3. Heat through and serve with lemon wedges.

Fish bobotie

A variation of the traditional meat bobotie.

6–8 servings

3 thick slices white bread, crusts removed
1 cup water
1 large onion, finely chopped
6 tablespoons (¾ stick) butter
3 pounds white fish (e.g., cod, halibut), filleted
½ cup lemon juice

2 tablespoons curry powder
1 teaspoon turmeric
1 teaspoon salt
dash of black pepper
3 tablespoons apricot jam
⅓ cup seedless raisins
⅓ cup slivered almonds
2+2 eggs
5 bay leaves or lemon leaves
¾ cup milk

1. Soak the bread in the water.
2. Sauté the onion in the butter, in a pan, for a few minutes.
3. Add the fish and lemon juice and simmer until cooked.
4. Remove the fish from the pan, flake coarsely and remove any bones. Set aside.
5. Add the curry powder, turmeric, salt, pepper, apricot jam, raisins and almonds to the pan and stir over low heat for a few minutes. Remove from the stove.
6. Add the bread and water to the pan together with two whisked eggs. Mix well.
7. Gently fold in the fish and scoop into a greased casserole dish.
8. Press the leaves into the mixture, leaving the tips protruding.
9. Whisk the remaining eggs and milk together.
10. Pour over the fish mixture and bake at 350° F for about 40 minutes, until the custard has set.
11. Remove the leaves and serve on yellow rice (page 107) with chutney (page 10, page 192), sliced banana, shredded coconut (unsweetened) and sambals (page 105, page 106).

Mock smoorsnoek

A braised mock snoek dish. Cape snoek (Thyrsites atun), an oily fish with a distinctive flavor, is native to South African waters.

4 servings

2 tablespoons oil
1 large onion, chopped
3 potatoes, peeled and cubed
2 6.7-ounce cans smoked herring, drained
1 cup water
1 small chili, seeded and chopped, optional
salt and pepper

1. Heat the oil in a frying pan and sauté the onion and potato until lightly browned.
2. Remove the skin and bones from the fish and flake.
3. Add the fish to the onion-potato mix and stir in the water and chili.
4. Cover with a lid and simmer for about 20 minutes, until the potato is soft.
5. Season to taste and serve on rice.

Notes

Smoked herring is a good substitute for smoked snoek in this recipe.

Fish and chip bake

4-6 servings

1 ½ pounds firm white fish (e.g., cod, halibut),
filleted and cut into serving-sized portions
¼ cup lemon juice
2 cups flavored potato or multigrain chips,
e.g., cheese & onion or chives with sour cream
2 large tomatoes, diced
1 14.5-ounce can asparagus cut spears,
drained and liquid retained

Cheese sauce
4 tablespoons (½ stick) butter
⅓ cup flour
salt and pepper
milk, made up to 2 cups with asparagus liquid
1 ½ cups grated sharp Cheddar cheese

1. Arrange the fish in a large, greased casserole dish and sprinkle with lemon juice.
2. Cover the fish with a layer of slightly crushed chips.
3. Layer the tomato and asparagus over the chips.
4. To make the cheese sauce, melt the butter in a saucepan and stir in the flour and seasoning.
5. Add the liquid and continue stirring over medium heat until the sauce is thick and smooth.
6. Add the cheese, mix and pour over the asparagus.
7. Bake at 350° F for 45 minutes, until the fish is cooked and the topping is lightly browned. Serve on rice.

Vegetarian bobotie

Variation of the traditional meat bobotie.

4 servings

1 tablespoon oil	½ cup seedless raisins
2 onions, chopped	4 medium carrots, coarsely
2 teaspoons curry powder	grated
1 teaspoon turmeric	2 cups chopped nuts, e.g.,
2 teaspoons apricot jam	macadamias and almonds
2 tablespoons chutney	1 egg, whisked
1 tablespoon vinegar	
1 cup crumbled day-old	3-4 bay leaves or lemon
brown bread	leaves
1 teaspoon Marmite (page 11)	1 egg, whisked with
dissolved in 1 cup hot water	¾ cup milk

1. Heat the oil in a saucepan and sauté the onion until glassy.
2. Add the curry powder, turmeric, apricot jam, chutney and vinegar and stir over medium heat for a minute or two to blend.
3. Add the bread and liquid and mix well. Remove from heat.
4. Stir in the raisins, carrot and nuts, together with the egg.
5. Scoop into a greased ovenproof casserole dish.
6. Press the leaves into the mixture at intervals, leaving the tips of the stalks protruding.
7. Cover with a lid and bake at 350° F for 25 minutes.
8. Pour the egg-milk mixture over the hot mixture and bake for a further 30-40 minutes, until the custard has set. Serve with yellow rice (page 107), sliced bananas, shredded coconut (unsweetened), chutney and sambals (page 105, page 106).

Notes

Instead of Marmite, add extra salt or replace the water with vegetable stock.

Chicken breyani

A traditional Cape Malay entrée adapted from Indian cuisine. This popular dish is served at special gatherings, such as birthdays, weddings and funerals.

6-8 servings

1 cup milk
3 tablespoons lemon juice
¼ teaspoon ground ginger
6 cloves garlic, crushed
2 tablespoons curry powder
½ teaspoon ground allspice
2 teaspoons ground cumin
1 teaspoon ground coriander
1 teaspoon turmeric
6 cloves
1 cinnamon stick
8 cardamom seeds
4 bay leaves
½ teaspoon salt

3 pounds boneless, skinless chicken pieces

3 cups rice
1 cup dried lentils
salt
½ teaspoon turmeric

½-1 cup oil
4 medium-small potatoes, peeled and quartered
2 large onions, thinly sliced
6 eggs, hard boiled, shelled and quartered

1. Put the milk and lemon juice into a large bowl and set aside for a few minutes for the milk to sour.
2. Add the ginger, garlic, curry powder, allspice, cumin, coriander, 1 teaspoon turmeric, cloves, cinnamon, cardamom, bay leaves and salt. Mix well.
3. Add the chicken pieces, mix to coat and set aside to marinate for at least two hours.
4. Add the rice to 5 cups of lightly salted boiling water. Boil for 15 minutes. Drain.
5. Rinse the lentils and add to 2 cups of lightly salted boiling water with ½ teaspoon turmeric. Boil for 15 minutes. Drain.
6. Heat the oil in a large, heavy-based saucepan and fry the potatoes until lightly browned on all sides. Remove from the saucepan and set aside.
7. Fry the onions in the same oil until lightly browned. Remove from the saucepan and set aside.
8. Spoon the chicken pieces with marinade into the saucepan with oil. Stir over high heat for a couple of minutes. Lower the temperature, cover with a lid and leave to simmer for 10-20 minutes.
9. Top with the potatoes, onions and eggs.
10. Cover with the lentils and then the rice.
11. Seal with foil and a tight-fitting lid.
12. Cook over high heat for a minute. Lower the temperature and simmer, or bake in the oven at 325° F, for an hour. Turn out onto a heated platter and serve with sambals (page 105, page 106).

Notes

The eggs can be reserved for garnishing and not baked with the breyani.

A Dutch oven is ideal for cooking breyani as it can be used on the stovetop as well as in the oven. There is less chance of the breyani burning if it is baked in the oven instead of over direct heat.

The ingredients can be layered into a slow cooker for the final cooking period.

Chicken pie

6-8 servings

4-6 ounces lean bacon, cut
into pieces
1 large onion, coarsely
chopped
1 pound skinless, boneless
chicken breast
1 ½ pounds skinless, boneless
chicken thighs
1-2 tablespoons oil
2 tablespoons flour

3 cloves garlic, crushed
2 ½ teaspoons dried thyme
1 cup boiling water
1 10 ¾-ounce can condensed
cream of mushroom soup
¾ teaspoon ground nutmeg
salt and pepper

1-2 sheets frozen puff pastry,
thawed

1. Sauté the bacon and onion for a few minutes in a large,
   heavy-based saucepan.
2. Add the chicken, with a little oil if necessary, and stir
   until lightly browned.
3. Sprinkle with the flour and add the garlic, thyme
   and water.
4. Cover with a lid and leave to simmer for about 45 minutes,
   until the chicken is very tender. Shred or cut into bite-
   sized pieces.
5. Add the soup and a little more boiling water if necessary.
   The mixture should be saucy but not watery.
6. Add the nutmeg and season to taste.
7. Transfer to a suitable casserole dish, wet the edges of the
   dish with iced water, and cover with a layer of pastry.
8. Double-edge the pastry round the edges, using cut-offs
   and iced water to join the layers. Crimp the edges lightly.
9. Use any remaining pieces of pastry to decorate the pie.
10. Make four or five slits in the pastry with a sharp knife to
    allow the steam to escape.
11. Bake at 400° F for 10 minutes, then lower the tempera-
    ture to 350° F for a further 30-40 minutes, until the crust
    is puffed up and lightly browned.

Notes

For an informal supper, drop scone dough (page 160) or dumplings (page 43) can be used as a topping instead of puff pastry.

This dish can also be prepared completely in the oven. Combine the first 8 ingredients in an ovenproof dish and bake at 350° F, covered, for about 90 minutes, until tender. Add the soup and enough boiling water to create a saucy consistency. Add the nutmeg and season to taste. Top with pastry as above.

Chutney chicken

4–6 servings

1 ½ pounds skinless, boneless chicken breasts or chicken tenders
1 large onion, coarsely chopped
oil for frying
¾ cup chutney (page 10, page 192)
3 cloves garlic, crushed
¾ cup mayonnaise

1. Cut the chicken into serving portions or bite-sized pieces.
2. Brown the chicken and onion in a little oil, in a heavy-based frying pan.
3. Mix the chutney and garlic together in a jug, and spoon over the chicken.
4. Lower the temperature and mix periodically to brown evenly and prevent burning.
5. Simmer for 20-30 minutes, until cooked.
6. Remove the chicken from the pan and place on a heated serving platter.
7. Add the mayonnaise to the pan and whisk to blend with the chutney. Heat to boiling point, pour over the chicken, and serve on rice.

Curried chicken

4 servings

3 tablespoons oil
1 tablespoon butter
1 onion, finely chopped

2 teaspoons curry powder
1 teaspoon ground ginger
1 teaspoon ground cinnamon
1 teaspoon ground cumin
1 teaspoon ground coriander
1 teaspoon turmeric

1 teaspoon paprika
½ cup water

1 pound skinless, boneless
chicken breast, portioned

3 tablespoons cornstarch
1 cup chicken stock
1 cup sour cream
salt and pepper to taste

1. Heat the oil and butter together in a pan and sauté the onion until glassy.
2. Add all the spices with the water and stir until blended.
3. Reduce the heat, add the chicken and coat with the spice mixture.
4. Cook the chicken over low heat on the stovetop for 10-15 minutes. Turn the chicken over and cook for another 10-15 minutes.
5. Measure the cornstarch into a bowl and add some of the stock to form a smooth, runny paste. Gradually whisk in the remaining stock and the sour cream.
6. Transfer the chicken from the pan to an ovenproof dish, leaving the spice mixture in the pan.
7. Add the stock mixture to the pan and stir, over medium heat, until the sauce thickens. Season to taste.
8. Pour the sauce over the chicken and cover.
9. Bake in the oven at 325° F for 40 minutes. Serve on rice.

Crumbed chicken

6 servings

1½ pounds, approximately, skinless, boneless chicken breasts
½ - ¾ cup mayonnaise
1 cup dried breadcrumbs

1. Using a sharp knife, slice each breast horizontally into 2-3 steak-like portions of about ¼ inch thick.
2. Coat with a thin layer of mayonnaise and then cover with breadcrumbs.
3. Arrange on a lightly greased baking tray or ovenproof platter.
4. Bake at 350° F for 25 minutes, until lightly browned and cooked through. If necessary, the chicken can be turned over and baked a little longer.

Notes

Whole chicken tenderloins can be used instead of sliced chicken breast. Use partially frozen breasts to simplify portioning.

Flaked almonds, blended to the consistency of breadcrumbs, can be used to coat the chicken portions instead of breadcrumbs.

For extra flavor, add Parmesan cheese to the breadcrumbs and/or a tablespoon of mustard to the mayonnaise.

Yogurt, or a combination of yogurt and mayonnaise, can be used instead of the mayonnaise.

Bobotie

A traditional, mildly curried ground lamb dish, topped with an egg and milk custard. Bobotie can also be made with beef or pork or a combination of ground meats.

6 servings

2 thick slices white bread, crusts removed
1½ cups water
1 tablespoon oil
1 large onion, finely chopped
2 pounds ground lamb
dash of black pepper

1 tablespoon mild curry powder
1 teaspoon turmeric
1½ teaspoons salt
2 tablespoons lemon juice
2 tablespoons apricot jam
3 tablespoons chutney (page 10, page 192)
⅓ cup seedless raisins
¼ cup dried apricots, quartered
⅓ cup slivered almonds
2+2 eggs
4-6 bay leaves or fresh lemon leaves
1 cup milk

1. Soak the bread in the water in a small bowl and mash together.
2. Heat the oil in a frying pan and sauté the onion until glassy.
3. Add the meat and stir over medium-high heat until brown and crumbly. Remove any excess fat.
4. Add the bread, with the pepper, to the meat and mix well.
5. Lower the temperature, cover with a lid and leave to simmer while mixing together the curry powder, turmeric, salt, lemon juice, jam and chutney in a cup.
6. Remove the meat mixture from the stovetop, and add the curry mix, raisins, apricots, almonds and 2 whisked eggs. Mix well.
7. Spoon into a lightly greased casserole dish and press the leaves into the meat, with the tips protruding.
8. Whisk the remaining eggs and the milk together in a jug, and pour over the meat.
9. Cover with a lid and bake at 350°F for 30 minutes. Remove the lid and bake for a further 10-20 minutes, until the custard topping has set. Serve on yellow rice (page 107) with chutney, sliced banana, shredded coconut (unsweetened), and sambals (page 105, page 106).

Notes

The custard will set more quickly if the bobotie mixture is hot when the egg-milk mix is poured over it.

Use only enough of the egg-milk mixture to cover the surface with a thin layer of custard. If the surface area is small, less of the egg-milk mixture will be needed. A thick layer of custard will take longer to set.

Tomato bredie

Tender lamb and tomato stew.

4–6 servings

3 tablespoons oil
1 large onion, coarsely chopped or wedged
2 pounds stewing lamb, cubed
3 tablespoons flour
1 14½-ounce can diced tomatoes
1 6-ounce can tomato paste
½ teaspoon sugar
2 teaspoons dried thyme
½ teaspoon ground nutmeg
¾ cup boiling water
3 potatoes, scrubbed or peeled, and cubed
1 teaspoon salt
¼ teaspoon black pepper

1. Heat the oil in a large, heavy-based saucepan and brown the onion and meat.
2. Sprinkle with flour and add the tomatoes, tomato paste, sugar, thyme, nutmeg and water.
3. Mix well, cover with a lid and leave to simmer for about 2 hours, stirring occasionally. Add more boiling water if necessary.
4. When the lamb is tender, add the potatoes, salt and pepper and simmer for a further 30 minutes, until the potatoes are soft. Adjust the seasoning and consistency of the sauce. Serve on rice.

Notes

This dish can be prepared in a slow cooker, according to the manufacturer's instructions, or in the oven, as follows: Put the oil and lamb into a casserole dish, sprinkle with flour and add the onion. Cover with a lid and bake at 350° F.

After about an hour, mix the tomatoes, tomato paste, sugar, thyme and nutmeg and pour over the meat. Add the boiling water, mix well and cover. Reduce oven temperature to 325° F and return to the oven for another hour, or until the meat is tender.

Add the potatoes, salt and pepper and bake for about 30 minutes, until the potatoes are soft.

Instead of stewing lamb, lamb neck, knuckle, shoulder, or leg chops can be used. Lamb neck and knuckle are very flavorsome, but have a low meat to bone ratio. Lamb shoulder is a less tender cut and requires longer cooking. Lamb leg chops are pricey, but tasty, and need less cooking time.

Braised lamb chops

4 - 6 servings

2 tablespoons oil	1 tablespoon Worcestershire
6-8 lamb leg or shoulder	sauce
chops	2 cloves garlic, crushed
2-3 tablespoons flour	pepper
1 large onion, cut into wedges	⅔ cup boiling water
1 teaspoon dried rosemary or	½ cup sour cream
3 sprigs fresh rosemary	salt

1. Place the oil and chops in a casserole dish. Sprinkle with flour and add the onion and rosemary.
2. Cover with lid and bake at 350° F for about an hour, until the meat is browned.
3. Add the Worcestershire sauce, garlic and pepper and stir in the water.
4. Return to the oven and bake at 325° F for another hour, or until the meat is tender.
5. Place the meat on a heated platter.
6. Stir the sour cream into the sauce and flavor to taste. Pour the sauce over the meat and serve.

Notes

A slow cooker can be used to prepare this dish. Follow the manufacturer's instructions.

Curried beef

4–6 servings

2 tablespoons oil
2 pounds stewing steak or
chuck, cubed
1 large onion, cut into
wedges
3 tablespoons flour
2 tablespoons curry powder
1 teaspoon turmeric
¼ cup tomato paste

½ cup red wine vinegar
½ cup apricot jam
¼ teaspoon sugar
1 teaspoon salt
¼ teaspoon black pepper
½-1 cup boiling water
2 large potatoes, scrubbed
or peeled, and cubed

1. Place the oil, beef and onion in a casserole dish.
2. Sprinkle with flour, mix, cover with lid and bake in the oven at 350° F for about an hour.
3. Mix the remaining ingredients, excluding the potatoes, and add to the meat. Mix carefully, to loosen the brown, crispy bits from the base. Cover and return to the oven, at 325° F, for another hour, or until the meat is tender.
4. Add the potato and return to the oven for about 30 minutes, until the potato is soft.
5. Adjust the consistency of the sauce by adding a little boiling water if necessary. Serve on rice.

Notes

To prepare on the stovetop, heat the oil in a heavy-based saucepan and brown the meat and onion. Sprinkle with flour and mix well. Add the remaining ingredients, excluding the potato, mix, cover and simmer for about 2 hours, until the meat is tender. Add a little boiling water if necessary. Add the potato cubes for the last 30 minutes of cooking. Adjust the flavoring and consistency of the sauce.

This dish can be prepared in a slow cooker. Follow the manufacturer's directions.

Hot Durban curry

6 servings

¼ cup oil
2 medium-large onions, finely chopped
3 large cloves garlic, crushed
1 teaspoon grated fresh ginger root
2 tablespoons hot curry powder
1½ tablespoons hot chili powder
½ teaspoon cayenne pepper
1 teaspoon dried cumin

2 pounds cubed lamb or beef
1 cinnamon stick
2 tablespoons apricot jam
1 tablespoon vinegar
¾ cup hot water
1 14.5-ounce can diced peeled tomatoes
¼ teaspoon sugar
2 medium-large potatoes, peeled and cubed
2 carrots, cut into rounds
salt and freshly ground black pepper to taste
cilantro leaves, chopped

1. Heat the oil in a heavy-based pan, cast-iron casserole or Dutch oven, and sauté the onions.
2. Add the garlic, ginger, curry, chili, cayenne and cumin and stir over medium heat for a couple of minutes.
3. Add the meat and stir over medium heat until coated with the spices.
4. Stir in the cinnamon stick, jam, vinegar and hot water and bring to the boil.
5. Cover with a tight-fitting lid and simmer, or place in the oven at 325° F, for 1½-2 hours, until the meat is tender.
6. Add the tomatoes, sugar, potatoes and carrots. Mix well, adding a little boiling water if necessary, and cook for another 40-50 minutes, until the potatoes are soft.
7. Adjust the flavor, garnish with cilantro and serve on rice with chutney (page 10, page 192) and sambals (page 105, page 106).

Notes
For a milder Durban curry, use mild curry and chili powders and just a pinch of cayenne pepper.

Oxtail stew

4–6 servings

¼ cup oil
3 pounds oxtail, cut into
joints and excess fat removed
2 onions, coarsely chopped
¼ cup flour
2 carrots, chunked
4 celery sticks with leaves,
sliced

pepper
3 bay leaves
6 whole cloves
1 cup boiling water
salt
1 pound baby jacket potatoes
½ pound baby carrots
¼ cup finely chopped parsley

1. Heat the oil in a heavy-based saucepan. Brown the oxtail, a few pieces at a time, and remove the meat from the saucepan.
2. Sauté the onion, return the meat to the saucepan, and sprinkle with flour.
3. Add the chunked carrots, celery, pepper, bay leaves, cloves and water. Stir to loosen the brown bits from the base.
4. Cover with a lid and simmer, or transfer to an ovenproof casserole and bake in the oven at 350° F, for 3-4 hours until the meat is very tender. Add boiling water as required; do not allow the stew to boil dry.
5. Remove the bay leaves and cloves, scoop off any fat and add salt to taste.
6. Add the potatoes and baby carrots to the stew and continue cooking for a further 30-40 minutes, until cooked.
7. Adjust the flavoring, sprinkle with parsley and serve on rice.

Notes

Stews or bredies usually taste better when served a day after the initial cooking.

Oxtail stew can be refrigerated, or frozen, before adding the baby vegetables. Remove any surface fat before reheating.

Steak and kidney pie

4-6 servings

3 tablespoons oil
2 pounds stewing steak or chuck, cubed
3 sheep kidneys, cleaned, skinned and diced
1 large onion, coarsely chopped
¼ cup flour
1 teaspoon salt
¼ teaspoon pepper
⅛ teaspoon ground cloves
2 bay leaves
boiling water
1 sheet frozen puff pastry, thawed

1. Heat the oil in a heavy-based saucepan and brown the meat, kidneys and onion.
2. Sprinkle with flour, salt, pepper and cloves.
3. Add the bay leaves, with ¾-1 cup water, and mix well.
4. Cover with a lid and simmer for 1½-2 hours, until the meat is tender. Add enough boiling water to create a saucy consistency. Remove the bay leaves and adjust the flavoring.
5. Transfer the stew to a suitable casserole bowl. Wet the edges of the bowl with iced water and cover with a layer of pastry.
6. Double-edge the pastry around the edges, using cut-offs and iced water to join the layers. Crimp the edges lightly.
7. Use any remaining pieces of pastry to decorate the pie.
8. Make four or five slashes in the pastry with a sharp knife to allow the steam to escape.
9. Bake at 400° F for 10 minutes, then lower the temperature to 350° F for a further 20-30 minutes, until the crust is puffed up and lightly browned.

Notes

For an informal supper, drop scone dough (page 160) or dumplings (page 43) can be used as a topping instead of puff pastry.

Instead of simmering the meat on the stovetop, it can be transferred to a suitable casserole dish, covered with a lid, and baked in the oven at 350° F until tender.

Monkeygland steak

Oven-baked steak (beef, not monkey!) in a zesty sauce.

3–4 servings

Marinade
3 tablespoons oil
2 medium onions, finely chopped
2 large cloves garlic, crushed
¼ cup tomato ketchup
¼ cup chutney (page 10, page 192)
2 teaspoons Worcestershire sauce
2 tablespoons wine vinegar
2 teaspoons dark brown sugar
1 tablespoon prepared mustard
1 ½ pounds beef sirloin or flank steak

½ cup hot water
2 teaspoons cornstarch, mixed with
2 tablespoons cold water

1. Mix the marinade ingredients together in a bowl and marinate the steak for at least 4 hours.
2. Remove meat from the marinade and transfer to a pre-heated oven pan. Set the marinade aside.
3. Bake, uncovered, at 400° F for 25 minutes.
4. Place the meat on a heated serving platter.
5. Make the sauce. Place the oven pan on the stovetop and add the marinade and hot water to the pan drippings. Bring to the boil, while stirring to loosen the brown bits from the base.
6. Stir in the cornstarch and simmer for a few minutes. Add a little water if the sauce is too thick. Serve the sauce with the sliced steak.

Curried mince

4 servings

1 tablespoon oil
1 onion, coarsely chopped
1 pound ground beef
3 cloves garlic, crushed
1 ½ tablespoons curry powder
1 teaspoon turmeric
1 teaspoon ground ginger
1 teaspoon ground allspice
½ teaspoon salt
pepper
3 tablespoons ketchup
3 bay leaves
½ cup boiling water
1 cup peas

1. Heat the oil in a frying pan and sauté the onion and mince until brown and crumbly.
2. Add the garlic, spices, salt, pepper, ketchup, bay leaves, water and peas and simmer for 20 minutes.
3. Remove the bay leaves and adjust the seasoning to taste.

Notes

Serve with vetkoek (page 35) or as a filling for bunny chow (page 38).

Frikadelle

Meatballs.

Yield: 16 large meatballs

2 thick slices bread, white or brown, crusts removed and soaked in
½ cup water
2 pounds ground beef
1 large onion, finely chopped
2 teaspoons dried thyme
1 ½ teaspoons salt
½ teaspoon pepper
1 teaspoon ground nutmeg
¼ cup tomato ketchup
2 eggs, whisked

1. Mix all the ingredients together in a bowl and shape lightly into about 16 meatballs.
2. Arrange in a single layer in a large, greased casserole dish and bake in the oven at 350° F for about 45 minutes, until cooked.

Notes

Meatballs can also be made with ground pork, lamb or turkey.

To create a saucy dish, cover the meatballs with a can of condensed soup (e.g., tomato or cream of mushroom) before baking.

Meatballs in cabbage leaves

Yield: 16 large cabbage parcels

16 frikadelle, uncooked (see page 74)
16 cabbage leaves
1 ½ cups beef or vegetable stock
ground nutmeg

1. Remove the outer leaves from a cabbage. Wash well, cut out the hard, stalky bits and steam in an inch of water for about 4 minutes, until just soft.
2. Once cool enough to handle, fold the leaves around the meatballs to form neat parcels.
3. Arrange in a single layer in a large greased, ovenproof casserole dish and add the stock.
4. Sprinkle with a little nutmeg.
5. Bake, uncovered, at 350° F for about an hour, until cooked.

Cottage pie

Also known as Shepherd's pie.

6-8 servings

1 tablespoon oil
2 pounds ground beef, pork or lamb, or a combination
1 medium onion, chopped
2 large cloves garlic, crushed
2 teaspoons dried marjoram
1½ teaspoons salt
½ teaspoon pepper
1 14½-ounce can diced tomatoes
¼ teaspoon sugar
¼ teaspoon ground nutmeg

Potato topping
4 medium potatoes, peeled and cut into chunks
2 tablespoons (¼ stick) butter
salt and pepper to taste
milk
1 egg, whisked
dried herbs

1. Heat the oil in a pan and brown the meat and onion. Remove any excess oil.
2. Add the remaining ingredients, mix, lower heat and simmer for about 15 minutes, while preparing the potato topping.
3. Boil the potatoes in a little water until most of the water has boiled away and the potatoes are soft.
4. Mash the potatoes with a fork or potato masher and add the butter and seasoning. An electric hand beater can be used to produce nice fluffy mashed potato.
5. If the potato is very dry, add a little milk and whisk in the egg until blended.
6. Scoop the meat mixture into a lightly greased casserole dish.
7. Top with the mashed potato and sprinkle with herbs.
8. Bake at 350° F for about 30-40 minutes, until lightly browned.

Notes

As an interesting variation, sweet potato can be used instead of potato.

Parmesan or Cheddar cheese and/or a little fresh parsley can be sprinkled on top instead of the dried herbs.

Oumie's pork chop casserole

3-4 servings

2 tablespoons oil
4-6 pork loin chops
2 tablespoons soy sauce
1 cup long grain rice
2 tablespoons (¼ stick) butter
1 clove garlic, crushed
1 14.5-ounce can diced and peeled tomato
2 tablespoons tomato ketchup
½ teaspoon salt
½ teaspoon sugar
warm water
1 large onion, thickly sliced
1 green pepper, seeded and sliced into broad rings or strips
thyme, fresh (chopped) or dried

1. Heat the oil in a frying pan and brown the chops on both sides.
2. Sprinkle the soy sauce over the chops. Remove the chops from the pan and set aside.
3. Add the rice and butter to the pan and brown slightly.
4. Mix the garlic, tomato, ketchup, salt and sugar in a large measuring jug. Add warm water to a volume of 2¼ cups (see Notes). Add to the rice, mix well and transfer to an ovenproof casserole dish.
5. Place the chops on top of the rice and arrange the onion and green pepper on the chops. Sprinkle liberally with thyme.
6. Cover and bake at 325° F for about an hour, until the rice is cooked.

Notes

Adjust the amount of liquid per cooking instructions for the rice.

Pork olives

Slices of pork rolled around a flavorsome, meaty filling.

4 servings

Filling
¼ pound ground pork
1 small onion, finely chopped
2 cloves garlic, crushed
pinch of salt
dash of black pepper
¼ teaspoon dried thyme

Dijon mustard
1 pound very thinly sliced pork sirloin or loin
4 large pickles (gherkins), thinly sliced, lengthwise
6 thin rashers of bacon, approximately 3 ounces
3-4 tablespoons flour
1 large onion, wedged
½ cup boiling water
1 4-ounce can sliced mushrooms

1. Mix the ground pork, finely chopped onion, garlic, salt, pepper and thyme together in a small mixing bowl.
2. Spread a thin layer of mustard on each slice of pork, and top with a slice of pickle, bacon and a spoon of ground pork mixture.
3. Fold the meat over the filling to form a 'sausage' (olive). The length of the olives will depend on the cut of meat.
4. Arrange the olives in a greased roasting pot or casserole, seam side down.

5. Sprinkle the meat with flour and add the remaining onion.
6. Cover with a lid and bake at 350° F for about an hour.
7. Carefully remove the olives from the roasting pot and, using a sharp knife, cut into pieces of 1½-2 inches in length.
8. Add the water and the mushrooms with brine to the roasting pot and stir to loosen the brown bits from the base of the pot.
9. Return the olives to the pot and mix carefully.
10. Cover with a lid and return to the oven for another 30-40 minutes at 325° F. Adjust the consistency of the gravy by adding a little boiling water, if necessary.

Notes

Thinly sliced beef sirloin can be used instead of pork. Breakfast sausage meat can be used as a filling instead of the above mixture. Olives can be made in advance and re-heated when needed, since they freeze well.

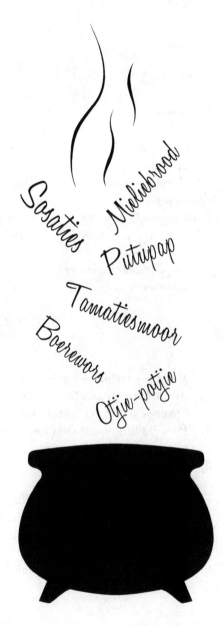

Sosaties Mieliebrood Putupap Tamatiesmoor Boerewors Otjie-potjie

Braais and Potjies

Sosaties

Kebabs.

Yield: 10-12

Marinade

1 small onion, finely chopped
2 tablespoons oil
¼ cup smooth apricot jam
2 tablespoons vinegar or
lemon juice
2 teaspoons brown sugar
4 teaspoons curry powder
½ teaspoon salt
¼ teaspoon black pepper
2 bay leaves

1½ pounds leg of lamb
meat, cut into 1-inch cubes
¼ pound mutton fat, cubed
(optional)

2 large onions, cut into
wedges and layers separated
¾ cup dried apricots
½ cup dried prunes, pitted
and halved

10-12 bamboo skewers

1. Mix the marinade ingredients in a bowl or plastic bag.
2. Add the lamb and fat, and mix well.
3. Cover/seal and refrigerate for 12-24 hours.
4. Pour boiling water over bamboo skewers and soak for about an hour before use. This reduces splintering.
5. At the same time, pour boiling water over the dried fruit and soak for about an hour. Drain.
6. Make the sosaties by threading the meat, onion, fat and dried fruit alternately onto the skewers.
7. Grill over medium heat, turning regularly to cook evenly and prevent burning.
8. Baste the sosaties with remaining marinade.

Chicken sosaties

Yield: 10-12

Marinade
1 small onion, finely chopped
3 tablespoons oil
1 tablespoon lemon juice
3 tablespoons honey
2 tablespoons soy sauce
2 cloves garlic, crushed
½ teaspoon salt
dash of black pepper
1 teaspoon dried thyme

1½ pounds (approximately) boneless and skinless chicken breast, cut into 1-inch cubes

2 large onions, cut into wedges and layers separated
1 large red pepper, cut into wedges
4 medium zucchini, cut into wedges or slices

10-12 bamboo skewers

1. Mix the marinade ingredients together in a bowl or plastic bag.
2. Add the chicken to the marinade.
3. Mix well, cover/seal and refrigerate for 12-24 hours.
4. Pour boiling water over the bamboo skewers and soak for at least an hour before use to minimize splintering.
5. Make the sosaties by threading the chicken, onion, pepper and zucchini alternately onto the skewers.
6. Grill over medium heat, turning periodically to cook evenly, while basting with remaining marinade.

Vegetable sosaties

1. Skewer a colorful combination of seasonal vegetables onto presoaked bamboo skewers.
2. Examples of suitable vegetables include baby jacket potatoes or portions of butternut, pumpkin or sweet potato, par-boiled; baby onions or onion, wedged; zucchini; green, red and yellow pepper, cut into wide strips; mushrooms; florets of cauliflower or broccoli; baby corn; and cherry tomatoes.
3. Grill over warm coals or broil in the oven.
4. Baste with melted butter or oil, flavored with garlic, lemon zest, and/or herbs.

Salad sosaties

1. For an attractive presentation of salad, spear portions of salad onto pre-soaked skewers.
2. Examples of suitable ingredients include varieties of lettuce, pineapple, cherry tomatoes, sundried tomatoes, peppers, zucchini, cucumber, pickles (gherkins), olives, apple, sugar snap peas, sweet onion, mushrooms, fresh basil, cubes of feta cheese, and marinated mozzarella balls.
3. Serve with salad dressing.

Fruit/dessert sosaties

1. Fruit sosaties make an attractive and light dessert.
2. Experiment with different flavor and color combinations, incorporating fruits such as cantaloupe, pears, mango, watermelon, kiwi fruit, litchis, apples, grapes, berries, pineapple, peaches and apricots.
3. Skewer and arrange on platters, decorated with grape leaves and/or mint. Serve with whipped cream or yogurt.

Vegetable parcels

1. Heavy duty aluminum foil squares, shiny side up.
2. 4-5 seasonal vegetables, such as baby potatoes, baby onions or wedges of onion, baby corn, mushrooms, young green beans, slivers of garlic, portions of butternut or pumpkin, florets of broccoli or cauliflower and chunks of sweet potato or yam, zucchini, tomato, carrot or eggplant.
3. Arrange a colorful and flavorsome combination of vegetables on the foil.
4. Top with a piece of plain or garlic butter and season to taste.
5. Wrap securely, to seal the contents.
6. Cook next to warm coals or over medium-high heat on a grill for about 45 minutes, until done.

Notes

Wrap whole potatoes or sweet potatoes/yams in their jackets, or onions, top-and-tailed but unpeeled, in a double layer of heavy duty foil, shiny side out. Place around the hot coals, turning periodically, for 30-45 minutes, until cooked.

Corn on the cob can also be cooked on the coals. Turn back the husks and strip away the silk. Wash the corn, pat dry and brush with melted butter. Pull the husks back into position and lay the cobs on the grill over hot coals. Grill for 15-20 minutes, turning frequently. Alternatively, strip the husks off the corn, brush with melted butter and wrap in heavy duty foil, shiny side out. Place around the hot coals, turning frequently, for 10-15 minutes, until cooked.

Putupap

Corn porridge, a staple food in South Africa, is often served at braais with tomato-onion mix or chakalaka (page 88). Somewhat similar to grits.

4-6 servings

2 cups water
½ teaspoon salt
1 tablespoon butter
2½ cups white or yellow cornmeal

1. Boil the water, salt and butter in a heavy-based saucepan. Slowly add the cornmeal, so that it forms a mound surrounded by boiling water.
2. Do not stir. Turn off the heat, cover and leave for 15 minutes.
3. Remove the lid and stir with a cutting motion to mix.
4. Using a fork, transfer the porridge to an ovenproof dish, so that it is loose and crumbly.
5. Cover with a lid and bake at 250° F for an hour.
6. Mix occasionally with a fork. If the pap (porridge) is very moist, remove the lid so that it can dry out slightly.

Notes

The porridge can be cooked entirely on the stovetop. However, due to the high ratio of cornmeal to water, it tends to stick to the base of the saucepan and burn very easily, unless the temperature is extremely low.

Krummelpap (crumbly porridge) can be made as above. However, use a 2:1 ratio of cornmeal to water. This mixture is very dry.

Tamatiesmoor

Tomato-onion mix.

4 servings

1 tablespoon oil
1 medium onion, chopped
1 14.5-ounce can diced tomatoes
½ 6-ounce can tomato paste
½ teaspoon sugar
¼ teaspoon ground nutmeg
½ teaspoon salt
dash of black pepper

1. Sauté the onion in oil until lightly browned. Add the remaining ingredients.
2. Mix, cover and simmer for about 15 minutes. Serve with putupap (page 86) and grilled meat.

Chakalaka

8-10 servings

3 tablespoons oil
1 medium-large onion, wedged
3 green chilies, seeded and finely chopped
1 green, red or yellow pepper, seeded and coarsely diced
3 medium carrots, pared and coarsely grated
1 small cauliflower rinsed and broken into florets
1 tablespoon curry powder
2 cloves garlic, crushed
2-4 tablespoons water
1 16-ounce can baked beans in tomato sauce
1 teaspoon salt
black pepper

1. Heat the oil in a frying pan. Add the onion, chili, pepper, carrot and cauliflower and stir over medium to high heat for 2-3 minutes. Sprinkle with the curry powder and mix.
2. Add the garlic, with a little water, to the vegetables and stir over medium heat for 3-4 minutes, until the vegetables are just soft.
3. Add the beans with the sauce, salt and pepper. Mix well to combine the ingredients and chill. Serve cold with putupap (page 86) and grilled meat.

Toasted cheese and tomato sandwiches

bread
butter
tomato, thinly sliced

onion, thinly sliced
salt and pepper to taste
grated Cheddar cheese

1. Butter the bread and make sandwiches with the remaining ingredients (buttered side out).
2. When the meat is just about ready, place the sandwiches on the grill over low heat and toast both sides until light brown on the outside and hot and melty inside.
3. Cut into portions with a pair of kitchen shears, which can also be used to cut the boerewors and check whether the steaks are done!

Griddle cakes

4-6 servings

2 cups flour
1 tablespoon baking powder

½ teaspoon salt
¼ cup oil
1 egg
water or milk

1. Mix the flour and salt in a bowl.
2. Measure the oil into a measuring jug, add the egg and top up to ⅔ cup with the liquid. Whisk.
3. Add the liquid ingredients to the dry ingredients.
4. Mix to form a pliable dough.
5. Shape into a square or rectangle of about 2½ inches thick and cut into 4-6 cakes.
6. Place on a hot grill over medium heat. Turn periodically to prevent burning. Serve with butter.

Garlic bread

Yield: 1 loaf

Garlic butter
½ cup (1 stick) butter, at room temperature
2-3 cloves garlic, crushed
salt to taste
chopped parsley (fresh or dried) or chives, optional

1 French loaf or baguette

1. Mix the garlic butter ingredients together.
2. Slice the bread, keeping the slices in order.
3. Spread garlic butter liberally between each slice and sandwich the slices back together.
4. Spread any remaining butter along the top crust and sprinkle with salt.
5. Wrap securely in aluminum foil, shiny side towards the bread, and heat in the oven at 350° for 15-20 minutes, until the butter has melted.

Mieliebrood

Sweet corn loaf.

Yield: 1 small loaf

2 cups flour
1 tablespoon baking powder
pinch of salt
1 tablespoon white sugar
1 egg, whisked
1 14.75-ounce can cream style corn

1. Mix the flour, baking powder, salt and sugar in a mixing bowl.
2. Using a spatula or knife, mix in the egg and corn with a light, cutting motion.
3. Scoop the mixture into a small, greased loaf tin (9 x 5 x 3 inches) and bake at 350° F for about an hour. Serve warm with butter.

Notes

This can also be made into 6-8 muffins. Spoon the dough into greased muffin pans and bake at 350° F for 20-30 minutes, until done.

Potjiekos

"Small pot food". Layers of meat, vegetables, herbs and spices stewed in a three-legged or flat-bottomed cast iron pot over a fire or hot coals.

There are many variations of potjiekos, and people enjoy creating their own versions of this dish. Annual potjiekos competitions, where families and friends compete to make the tastiest potjie ("small pot"), are popular cultural events. A batch of potjiekos typically takes several hours to prepare, allowing plenty of time for socializing and merriment.

Potjiekos evolved as a method to cook venison and other available game (e.g., rabbits, guinea fowl and warthogs). Nowadays, lamb, pork, beef and ostrich are commonly used. Tougher, less expensive cuts of meat are suitable for this form of preparation. Fish, chicken and vegetarian potjies are also popular.

The following recipes use the traditional method of potjiekos preparation. Alternatively, layer the ingredients in an ovenproof pot, Dutch oven or casserole and bake in the oven at 350° F, until tender, or prepare in a slow cooker, as per manufacturer's instructions.

Tomato-chutney chicken potjie

6-8 servings

2 tablespoons (¼ stick) butter
2 tablespoons oil
2 chickens, portioned
1 large onion, chopped

2 cloves garlic, crushed
salt and pepper
herbs, fresh or dried
1 cup tomato ketchup
1 cup chutney (page 10, page 192)
2 cups Coca-Cola

1. Heat the butter and oil in a flat-bottomed pot or potjie and brown the chicken pieces and onion. Add the garlic.
2. Season to taste.
3. Mix the ketchup, chutney and cola, and pour it over the chicken.
4. Mix well, cover and simmer over slow coals for 2-3 hours, until the chicken is tender. Stir periodically so that it does not burn.

Chicken and yogurt potjie

6-8 servings

Marinade
2 cups plain yogurt
2 cups dry white wine
1 medium onion, finely chopped
2 cloves garlic, crushed
2 teaspoons dried thyme
2 teaspoons fresh lemon zest
1 teaspoon black pepper
4-5 pounds chicken pieces
¼ cup oil
2 green peppers, seeded and sliced

4 carrots, pared and cut into rounds
1 large onion, coarsely chopped
6 medium potatoes, quartered
1 pound green beans
1 10½-ounce can condensed cream of mushroom soup

1 tablespoon cornstarch mixed with
2 tablespoons cold water
salt and pepper

1. Mix the marinade ingredients together in a bowl and add the chicken.
2. Mix to coat the chicken and set aside in a cool place for at least 8 hours.
3. Remove the chicken from the marinade, and set the marinade aside.
4. Heat the oil in a potjie or a flat-bottomed pot and fry the chicken until lightly browned.
5. Arrange the chicken on the base of the pot and cover with the marinade.
6. Layer the vegetables, starting with the peppers on top of the marinade and ending with the mushroom soup.
7. Cover with a lid and cook over medium heat for about 3 hours. Do not stir.
8. Before serving, mix the chicken and vegetable layers. Thicken the sauce with a little cornstarch, if necessary, and adjust the seasoning.

Otjiepotjie

Pork shin potjie.

4-6 servings

½ pound bacon, cut into pieces
2 tablespoons oil
3-4 pounds pork shin
1 large onion, chopped
1 green pepper, seeded and chopped
1 large clove garlic, chopped
1 6-ounce can tomato paste
1 cup boiling water
½ teaspoon sugar
salt and pepper
1 pound cabbage, shredded
½ teaspoon ground nutmeg
1 leek, sliced
6 medium potatoes, cubed
4 carrots, cut into rounds
3 celery sticks, sliced
1 pound green peas

1. Brown the bacon lightly in a potjie or a flat-bottomed pot. Add some oil if necessary. Remove the bacon from the pot and set aside.
2. Brown the shin, remove it from the pot and set aside.
3. Sauté the onion, pepper and garlic in the pot. Add the tomato paste, water and sugar and mix well.
4. Stir in the shin and bacon and season with salt and pepper.
5. Simmer for an hour over medium coals. Add a little boiling water if necessary.
6. Add the cabbage to the pot and sprinkle with nutmeg. Layer the leek, potato, carrot, celery and peas on top of the cabbage.
7. Cover with a lid and cook over medium coals for 1-2 hours, until the vegetables are cooked and the meat is tender.

Boerewors

Farmers' sausage.

3 pounds boneless beef
3 pounds boneless pork
1 pound pork fat or bacon
1 ½ tablespoons salt
1 ½ tablespoons ground
coriander
1 teaspoon pepper

1 teaspoon ground cloves
1 ½ teaspoons ground nut-
meg
½ cup brown vinegar

3-4 ounces sausage casings,
soaked in lukewarm water
for 30 minutes before use

1. Remove any sinews from the meat and cut the meat into
   1-inch cubes.
2. Mix the salt and spices.
3. Layer the meat in a large glass, earthenware or enamel
   bowl or basin, and sprinkle each layer liberally with
   spices and vinegar. Set aside for about an hour.
4. Dice half the fat into ⅛-inch cubes. Partially freezing
   the fat will simplify the dicing. If bacon is used, finely
   slice the entire amount.
5. Coarsely mince the meat and the remaining fat. Add
   the diced fat and any remaining vinegar and spices. Mix
   lightly but thoroughly.
6. Fill the casings loosely.
7. Refrigerate and allow the flavors to blend for a day or
   two before cooking.

Notes

For extra flavor and authenticity, roast, grind and sift 3 ½
tablespoons of whole coriander seeds, and use instead of the
ground coriander.

Traditionally, the sausage is not twisted into individual
links, but is coiled, as one long sausage, on the grill.

There are a number of specialty South African stores
where authentic, South African sausage can be purchased.
In addition to boerewors, droëwors (dried sausage) can
sometimes be found, along with biltong (spiced, dehydrated
meat; somewhat reminiscent of jerky).

Monkeygland sauce

A sweet-sour accompaniment for steak, hamburgers and chicken.

Yield: 1 cup

3 tablespoons oil
1 medium onion, finely chopped
2 cloves garlic, crushed
¼ cup tomato ketchup
¼ cup chutney (page 10, page 192)
1 tablespoon Worcestershire sauce
2 tablespoons red wine vinegar
2 teaspoons brown sugar
1 tablespoon prepared mustard
⅓ cup water

1. Heat the oil in a saucepan and sauté the onion for a few minutes.
2. Add the remaining ingredients and simmer for 5 minutes.

Slaphakskeentjies

Armadillo potatoes

Sousboontjies

Apple sambal

Bubble and squeak

Salads & Sides

Slaphakskeentjies

"Little limp heals"; tender young onions in a sweet-sour sauce. Perhaps the name refers to the heel-shaped onion imprints in the sauce, or possibly the flavor that leaves one feeling 'weak at the knees' or 'limp at the ankles'!

4-6 servings

1 pound small, young onions or boiler onions
½-1 cup water
½ teaspoon salt

Sauce
2 eggs
2 tablespoons sugar
½ teaspoon salt
½ teaspoon ground mustard
⅓ cup white wine vinegar
¼ cup water

1. Peel the onions. See note below.
2. Boil the onions in water, with salt, for 10-12 minutes, until just soft. Do not overcook.
3. Drain well.
4. Make the sauce by whisking all the ingredients together in a double boiler or a small bowl over boiling water. When the sauce is cooked, it will thicken slightly and coat the back of a metal spoon.
5. Put the onions into a glass bowl and cover with the sauce. Serve warm, cold or at room temperature.

Notes

To peel onions easily, put them into a bowl and cover them with boiling water. Drain after 10 minutes, top and tail the onions, and squeeze them out of their skins.

This sauce complements young green beans that have

been boiled for about 10 minutes in a little salted water and drained. Sprinkle with toasted almonds and serve warm or cold.

Alternate method for making the sauce:

1. Whisk the eggs in a small bowl.
2. Heat the remaining ingredients in a small saucepan to boiling point.
3. Slowly add the boiling liquid to the egg, stirring all the time.
4. Return to the saucepan and stir over low heat until the sauce thickens, and coats the back of a metal spoon.

Sousboontjies

Saucy, sweet-sour dried bean salad.

4–6 servings

1 cup pinto beans
4-4½ cups water
2 tablespoons dark brown sugar
¼ cup red wine vinegar
½ teaspoon salt

1. Rinse the beans and soak them overnight in 2 cups of water, in a heavy-based saucepan.
2. Add 2 more cups of water and boil for 1-2 hours, until the beans are soft. Add more water if necessary.
3. Add the remaining ingredients and simmer for 5-10 minutes.
4. Once the beans have cooled down, the sauce will thicken. If watery, mash some of the beans to thicken the sauce further.

Three bean salad

8-10 servings

1 14½-ounce can green beans
1 15-ounce can butter beans
1 16-ounce can navy beans or
baked beans in tomato sauce
½ cup sugar
½ teaspoon ground mustard

½ teaspoon salt
½ cup oil
½ cup wine vinegar
2 teaspoons dried basil
1 large onion, chopped
1 small green pepper, seeded
and diced

1. Place all the beans in a colander and rinse under cold, running water. Set aside to drain.
2. Mix the sugar, mustard and salt in a large bowl and stir in the oil and vinegar. Continue stirring until the sugar dissolves.
3. Add the beans, basil, onion and pepper.
4. Mix, cover and refrigerate for at least a couple of hours before serving.

Curried dried fruit salad

4-6 servings

1 pound dried fruit (e.g.,
peaches, pears, apricots,
stoned prunes, raisins)
1 tablespoon oil
1 large onion, chopped
1 large clove garlic, crushed
¼ teaspoon salt
1 tablespoon mild curry
powder

1 teaspoon turmeric
½ teaspoon ground ginger
2 tablespoons apricot jam
1 tablespoon flour
¼ cup lemon juice
½ cup water

1. Place the fruit in a bowl and cover it with boiling water. Steep for a few hours at room temperature, or heat to boiling point, turn off the heat and cover with a lid until the curry sauce is made.
2. Heat the oil in a frying pan and sauté the onion until glassy. Add the garlic, salt, spices, jam and flour.
3. Stir over medium heat and slowly add the lemon juice and water. Continue stirring until the sauce thickens.
4. Drain the fruit and add it to the curry sauce. Heat to boiling point and simmer for 3-5 minutes. Scoop the salad into an attractive bowl and serve, warm or cold, with grilled or roast meat.

Curried peach salad

8-10 servings

1 tablespoon oil
1 large onion, coarsely chopped
2 teaspoons curry powder
1 teaspoon turmeric
½ teaspoon salt
½ cup white wine vinegar
1 29-ounce can yellow cling peach slices, in heavy syrup

1. Heat the oil in a small frying pan and sauté the onion until glassy.
2. Stir in the curry powder, turmeric and salt.
3. Mix in the vinegar and simmer for a few minutes.
4. Stir in the peach slices and about half of the syrup. Chill for at least 24 hours before serving.

Quick bean salad

3-4 servings

1 small onion, finely chopped
1 small green pepper, seeded and diced
1 16-ounce can baked beans in tomato sauce, drained but
not rinsed
3 tablespoons mayonnaise
¼ cup chutney, hot or mild (page 192)
freshly ground black pepper

1. Mix all the ingredients together and chill before serving.

Potato salad

6-8 servings

6 medium potatoes
1½ cups mayonnaise
¾ cup milk, approximately
1 large onion, chopped
½ cup chopped fresh parsley
4 eggs, hard boiled, shelled
and coarsely chopped
salt and pepper

1. Wash the potatoes. Boil them, in their jackets, in a few
    inches of water, until cooked but still firm (approximately
    20 minutes).
2. Drain and allow the potatoes to cool slightly before
    removing their skins.
3. Whisk the mayonnaise and milk together. The amount
    of milk needed depends on the consistency of the
    mayonnaise used. It should pour easily.
4. Pour a little of the mayonnaise mixture into the base of
    an attractive bowl.
5. Cover with a layer of sliced potato, some onion, parsley,
    egg, salt and pepper.

6. Cover with a layer of mayonnaise.
7. Repeat the layers, ending with mayonnaise.
8. Garnish with parsley and egg or a dash of paprika. Cover and refrigerate.

Notes

Potato salad should not be dry; add a little more mayonnaise if necessary.

Copper penny salad

Carrot rounds in a tomato vinaigrette.

8-10 servings

2 pounds carrots, pared and cut into rounds
2 medium onions, thinly sliced and separated into rings
1 small green pepper, seeded and sliced
1 14½-ounce can tomato soup

½ cup vinegar
½ cup oil
½ cup sugar
2 teaspoons Worcestershire sauce
1 teaspoon prepared mustard
¼ teaspoon salt
¼ teaspoon pepper

1. Bring an inch of water in a saucepan to a fast boil.
2. Add the carrots and boil rapidly for about 5 minutes. Drain and rinse under cold water. The carrots must not be soft.
3. Combine the carrot, onion and green pepper in an attractive bowl.
4. Mix the remaining ingredients in a small saucepan, heat to boiling point, and simmer for 5 minutes.
5. Pour the hot sauce over the vegetables and mix.
6. Refrigerate when cool and leave for at least a couple of hours before serving.

Carrot and pineapple salad

6- 8 servings

3 large carrots, washed and pared
1 small pineapple, peeled
pinch of salt
orange juice, approximately ½ cup

mint leaves, optional

1. Grate the carrots and pineapple and put into an attractive bowl.
2. Add the salt and as much orange juice as the salad will hold without being too wet.
3. Mix, cover and chill. Garnish with mint leaves before serving.

Butternut salad

A cleansing health salad with an unexpected mango-like flavor.

6-8 servings

1 small butternut, peeled and seeded
1 small pineapple, peeled
½-1 cup fresh orange juice
pinch of salt

1. Coarsely grate the raw butternut and pineapple.
2. Combine in a bowl and stir in the orange juice and salt.
3. Cover and chill for several hours or overnight before serving.

Cucumber sambal

Relish.

Yield: 2 cups

1 small English cucumber, with or without skin
½ teaspoon salt
1 small red pepper, finely diced
1 small onion, finely chopped
1 clove garlic, crushed
2 tablespoons red wine vinegar
½ teaspoon sugar

1. Coarsely grate the cucumber.
2. Put it into a colander or sieve, sprinkle with salt and set aside to drain for 5-10 minutes.
3. Mix the remaining ingredients in a bowl.
4. Squeeze the excess liquid from the cucumber before adding it to the mixed ingredients.
5. Mix, cover and refrigerate. Allow the flavors to blend and mellow for a couple of hours or overnight. Serve cold with curries or as a side dish with stews.

Apple sambal

A tangy relish.

Yield: 1½ cups

1 tart green apple (e.g.,
Granny Smith), coarsely
grated with peel
¼ teaspoon salt
½ small onion, finely chopped

1 small chili, seeded and diced
1 tablespoon red wine vinegar
¼ teaspoon sugar

1. Mix all the ingredients in a bowl.
2. Chill for at least a couple of hours, or overnight, so that
   the flavors blend. Serve as an accompaniment to curry.

Tomato sambal

A sweet-sour relish.

Yield: 1½ cups

2 large tomatoes, skinned
and diced
1 small onion, chopped
2 small chilies, seeded and
chopped

1 teaspoon sugar
¼ cup red wine vinegar
1 tablespoon oil
salt and pepper

cilantro leaves, chopped

1. Put the tomato, onion and chili into an attractive bowl.
2. Mix the sugar, vinegar and oil and pour over the salad.
   Season to taste.
3. Chill for a couple of hours, or overnight, so that the
   flavors can mellow.
4. Mix in the cilantro just before serving as an accompaniment to curries, meat or fish.

Yellow rice

Geelrys, also known as borrierys (turmeric rice), begrafnisrys (funeral rice) or vendusierys (possibly referring to large stock auctions where food was served). People travelled great distances to attend funerals and auctions, as the farms were large and spread out. A substantial meal was generally served before the long homeward journey, and yellow rice typically formed part of this fare.

6-8 servings

2 cups white rice
1 teaspoon salt
1 tablespoon sugar
2 teaspoons turmeric
½ cup seedless raisins
1 cinnamon stick
2 tablespoons (¼ stick) butter
boiling water, approximately 4 cups, according to specifications on the rice package

1. Put all the ingredients into a saucepan and bring to boil.
2. Cover and simmer until the water is absorbed.
3. Remove the cinnamon stick, fluff the rice with a fork and serve.

Notes

Rice can also be cooked in a covered ovenproof dish in the oven at 350° F for about an hour.

Armadillo potatoes

A unique way to prepare baked potatoes.

4-6 servings

6 medium potatoes
8 tablespoons (1 stick) butter, melted
2 cloves garlic, crushed
⅛ teaspoon salt
⅛ teaspoon pepper

½-¾ cup finely grated Parmesan cheese

1. Wash, dry and cut the potatoes in half, lengthwise.
2. Cut out about 6 wedges across the width of the rounded sides of the potato halves.
3. Arrange the potatoes in a large, greased ovenproof dish, flat side down.
4. Mix the butter, garlic, salt and pepper in a jug and coat the potatoes.
5. Sprinkle with cheese.
6. Bake the potatoes, uncovered, at 350° F for about an hour, until they are lightly browned and cooked through. Baste periodically with butter from the dish.

Notes

The potatoes can be par-cooked in the microwave before baking. This will shorten the cooking time considerably.

If available, brown onion soup powder can be sprinkled over the potatoes with the melted butter instead of garlic, seasoning and cheese.

Potato bake

4-6 servings

1 ½ pounds potato, peeled and thinly sliced
1 tablespoon butter
2 large onions, thinly sliced
2 large cloves garlic, crushed
½ cup fresh cream
½ cup sour cream
salt and pepper

1. Place the potato in a colander, rinse under cold, running water and pat dry.
2. Melt the butter in a frying pan and sauté the onion until glassy.
3. Mix the garlic, creams and seasoning in a bowl. Add the potato and mix to coat.
4. Layer the potato mixture and the onion in an ovenproof casserole dish.
5. Cover with a lid and bake at 325° F for 1 ½-2 hours until the potato is cooked.
6. Remove the lid and increase the oven temperature to 400° F. Bake until lightly browned.

Bubble and squeak

A traditional English dish of sautéed cabbage, potato and onion. Some ascribe the origin of the name to the popping and hissing sound made by the vegetables while they cook.

4-6 servings

2 large potatoes, peeled and quartered
1 small cabbage, finely shredded
1 medium onion, coarsely chopped
2 tablespoons (¼ stick) butter
salt
freshly ground black pepper
ground nutmeg

1. Steam or boil the potatoes in a little water until just soft. Drain and dice.
2. Steam or boil the cabbage over medium-high heat, in very little water, for 10 minutes.
3. Heat the butter in a frying pan and sauté the onion until glassy. Add the potato.
4. Drain the cabbage and add to the onion-potato.
5. Season with salt and pepper to taste.
6. Mix, cover and simmer for 10 minutes.
7. Sprinkle with nutmeg and serve.

Notes

Traditionally, cold, leftover vegetables (e.g., cabbage, onion and carrot) were chopped and fried in a pan together with mashed potato, until heated through and slightly browned. Often, leftover meat from the Sunday roast was also added.

Vegetable curry

4 servings

1 medium-sized eggplant
salt
1 tablespoon oil
1 medium onion, cut into
wedges
6 ounces, approximately,
cauliflower florets
1 green pepper, seeded and
cut into wedges
2-3 medium-small zucchini,
thickly sliced
1 green chili, seeded and
chopped
2 large cloves garlic, crushed
2 teaspoons curry powder

1 teaspoon ground coriander
1 teaspoon ground cumin
½ teaspoon turmeric
½ teaspoon chili powder
1 teaspoon salt
black or cayenne pepper

¼ cup cilantro leaves,
chopped

1. Cut the eggplant into cubes and place in a colander.
   Sprinkle with salt and set aside for 10-15 minutes. Rinse
   under cold, running water and pat dry.
2. Heat the oil in a heavy-based pan and sauté the onion
   and cauliflower for about 1 minute.
3. Add the eggplant, pepper, zucchini and chili and stir-fry
   over medium-high heat for 2-3 minutes. Add a few tablespoons of water if necessary.
4. Add the garlic and sprinkle with curry powder, coriander,
   cumin, turmeric, chili powder, salt and pepper. Mix well.
5. Cover with a lid and simmer for 5-10 minutes, until the
   vegetables are just cooked.
6. Fold in the cilantro leaves before serving hot or cold.

Butternut in sour cream

4-6 servings

1 medium butternut, peeled, seeded and diced
freshly ground pepper
1 cup sour cream
¼ cup olive oil
1 large clove garlic, crushed
½ teaspoon curry powder
½ teaspoon ground cumin
½ teaspoon salt
2 tablespoons finely chopped chives or green onions

1. Arrange the butternut on the base of an ovenproof
    platter, and sprinkle generously with pepper.
2. Mix the remaining ingredients together in a measuring
    jug and pour over the butternut.
3. Cover with a lid or foil and bake at 350° F for about
    50 minutes.
4. Remove the lid and bake, uncovered, for a further
    20-30 minutes, until soft and lightly browned.

Candied carrots

4 servings

½ pound carrots, peeled and julienned
¼ cup water
1 tablespoon butter
2 tablespoons sugar
salt

1. Par-boil the carrots in the water in a covered pan for
    about 5 minutes. Do not drain.

2. Add the remaining ingredients and cook, uncovered, over low heat for 20-30 minutes, mixing or shaking the pan periodically, to ensure that the carrots do not burn.

Braised carrots

Traditionally, vegetables were simmered for many hours with onion and potato on a back plate of the wood-burning stove.

4-6 servings

2 tablespoons (¼ stick) butter
1 onion, coarsely chopped
¾ pound carrots, peeled and cut into rounds
1 potato, diced
½ cup water
salt and pepper

1. Melt the butter in a saucepan, and sauté the onion, carrot and potato until lightly browned.
2. Add the water, stir, cover with a lid and simmer until the vegetables are soft.
3. Season to taste.

Notes
Sliced green beans were often cooked as above, with a good dash of pepper added.

Sticky pumpkin or butternut

4-6 servings

1 pumpkin or butternut, peeled, seeded and cubed
1 cinnamon stick
4 tablespoons (½ stick) butter
¼ cup honey or golden syrup
1 tablespoon lemon juice

1. Put the pumpkin and cinnamon into a casserole dish.
2. Melt the butter with the honey, add the juice, and pour
    over the pumpkin.
3. Cover with a lid and bake at 350° F for 50-60 minutes,
    until almost soft.
4. Remove the lid, baste with the liquid and bake,
    uncovered, for another 15-20 minutes, until dry and
    lightly browned.

Glazed onions

8-10 servings

1 pound boiler onions
¾ cup water
½ teaspoon salt
2 tablespoons (¼ stick) butter
1 tablespoon brown sugar

3 tablespoons chopped chives

1. Peel the onions. See Notes.
2. Put the onions, water and salt into a small frying pan.
3. Heat to boiling point, cover with a lid, and boil for about
    10 minutes.

4. Add the butter and sugar and continue boiling, uncovered, until most of the liquid has evaporated.
5. Turn the heat down a little so that the onions do not burn. Stir the onions, or shake the pan, so that they glaze evenly on all sides.
6. When the onions are glazed and tender, sprinkle them with chives and serve hot.

Notes

To peel onions easily, put them into a bowl and cover them with boiling water. Drain after 10 minutes, top and tail the onions, and squeeze them out of their skins.

Glazed sweet potato

4-6 servings

¼ cup sugar
1 tablespoon butter
¼ cup water
1 pound sweet potato or yam, peeled and cut into thick French fries
1 tablespoon lemon juice
zest of one lemon
salt

1. Heat the sugar and butter in a saucepan over medium heat for about 5 minutes, until the sugar caramelizes. Watch carefully, as it could easily burn.
2. Remove from the heat and slowly mix in the water.
3. Add the remaining ingredients, mix and return to the stovetop.
4. Cover with a lid and simmer until the sweet potato is cooked.
5. If necessary, increase the heat to reduce any excess liquid before serving.

Mock gem squash

Gem squash is a green-skinned summer squash of delicate tex-
ture and flavor that is commonly grown in South Africa. Boiled
in a little lightly salted water, the skin and pips of baby/young
gems can be eaten. As the gem squash matures, the skin thickens
and the pips become hard. The marrow of the squash changes
from light to dark yellow and becomes more fibrous in texture.

4-6 servings

1 acorn squash, quartered, with seeds and fibers removed
2 tablespoons (¼ stick) butter
salt
sugar
ground cinnamon

1. Boil the squash in a saucepan with about an inch of
   water, until soft.
2. When cool enough to handle, remove the skin from
   the flesh.
3. Mash the flesh with a fork and put it into an ovenproof bowl.
4. Mix in the butter, salt and sugar to taste.
5. Sprinkle with cinnamon.
6. Bake at 350° F for about 30 minutes before serving.

Red cabbage with apple

Colorful side dish of German origin.

6 servings

1 small red cabbage, finely shredded
1 cup boiling water
¼ cup vinegar
2 Granny Smith apples, peeled and diced
2 tablespoons dark brown sugar
1 teaspoon salt
pepper
½ teaspoon ground cinnamon

1. Place the cabbage, water and vinegar in a saucepan and boil for 10 minutes.
2. Add the remaining ingredients. Mix, cover and simmer for 45-50 minutes, until the cabbage is soft.

Trifle

Telephone pudding

Japie se gunsteling

Buttermilk pudding

Jelly whip-whip

Desserts

Baked custard

4-6 servings

2 cups milk
2 eggs
4 egg yolks
3 tablespoons sugar
½ teaspoon vanilla extract
ground nutmeg or cinnamon

1. Heat the milk in a saucepan to just below boiling point.
2. Whisk the eggs, yolks, sugar and vanilla together.
3. Gradually add the hot milk to the mixture, while whisking.
4. Pour into an ovenproof bowl or six ramekins.
5. Sprinkle with nutmeg.
6. Place the bowl or ramekins in a water bath (large Pyrex dish or deep baking pan containing 1-2 inches of warm water) and bake at 350° F for 30-45 minutes, until set.

Notes

Unused egg whites can be used to make two pavlova shells or mini pavlovas (page 124).

Guava-marshmallow pudding

4 servings

1 cup marshmallows, cut into pieces
1 15-ounce can guavas (page 11), drained and cut into
little pieces
1 cup heavy cream, whipped

1. Melt the marshmallows in a bowl set over boiling water,
   or in a microwave.
2. Fold in the guavas and cream.
3. Chill before serving.

Notes

Guavas can be replaced with pears or other fruit.
   To facilitate the cutting of the marshmallows, use
kitchen shears dipped in boiling water.

Mango supreme

mango, peeled and sliced
Greek yogurt
brown sugar

1. Arrange the mango in an attractive glass bowl.
2. Top with a thick layer of yogurt.
3. Sprinkle liberally with sugar.
4. Cover and chill for at least 8 hours before serving.

Trifle

4-6 servings

Custard

3+¼ cups milk
2 tablespoons cornstarch   ½-¾ cup apricot or berry jam
¼ cup sugar   ½ cup sherry
pinch of salt
3 eggs   1 cup heavy cream
1 teaspoon vanilla extract   2 tablespoons sugar
                                                      ¼ teaspoon vanilla extract
1 sponge cake or loaf (page
155)   cherries, fresh or glacé

1. Make the custard by heating 3 cups of milk in a saucepan to just below boiling point.
2. Mix the cornstarch, sugar and salt in a bowl.
3. Whisk the eggs with the remaining ¼ cup of milk and
   gradually add to the dry ingredients, while whisking, to
   form a smooth paste.
4. Pour the hot milk over this paste, while stirring.
5. Return the milk mixture to the saucepan and stir over
   low heat until the custard thickens and coats the back of
   a metal spoon.
6. Remove from the stove, add the vanilla and set aside.
7. Cut the sponge into 1-inch slices and spread with jam. Cut
   into 1-inch blocks.
8. Pour a little of the warm custard onto the base of an
   attractive glass bowl.
9. Top with a layer of sponge blocks.
10. Moisten the sponge with a little sherry.
11. Cover with a layer of custard.
12. Repeat the layers, ending with custard.
13. Whip the cream with the sugar until stiff. Fold in the
    vanilla.
14. Top the trifle with cream, either piped or spread.
15. Garnish with cherries and refrigerate.

Notes

A Swiss roll (page 152) can be used instead of a sponge cake or loaf and jam. Boudoir biscuits are often used in trifles instead of sponge cake. A large and elaborate dessert can be made by adding fruit, jelly and nuts.

Trifle must be moist. Add extra fruit juice, sherry and custard if necessary.

Microwave fudge

2 cups ultrafine sugar
8 tablespoons (1 stick) butter
1 14-ounce can full cream sweetened condensed milk
1 teaspoon vanilla extract

1. Place the sugar, butter and condensed milk in a 2-quart microwave-safe bowl.
2. Microwave on full power for 2 minutes.
3. Add the vanilla, stir and return to the microwave.
4. Microwave on full power for 8-10 minutes. The fudge should be golden brown in color.
5. Remove from the microwave and beat well.
6. Pour into a greased dish.
7. Leave to cool slightly and then cut lightly into squares.
8. Break into pieces when cool.

Notes

The bowl must be large enough to contain the bubbling mixture. The cooking time may vary slightly with different microwaves and at different altitudes.

Pavlova

A meringue-like dessert decorated with whipped cream and fruit.

Yield: two 9-inch rounds

4 egg whites
pinch of salt
1¼ cups white sugar
¼ cup cornstarch
2 teaspoons white vinegar

Topping/filling
whipped heavy cream, with sugar and vanilla to taste
ice cream or custard
seasonal fruits (e.g., berries, kiwi fruit, passion fruit)

1. Use a 9-inch dinner plate as a template to draw two circles on a sheet of parchment paper or foil with a food-safe marker. Place on a baking sheet and grease lightly. Dust with a little cornstarch and set aside.
2. Whisk the egg whites with salt until frothy.
3. Slowly add the sugar, initially a spoon at a time, while beating continuously until very stiff.
4. Sift the cornstarch over the whites and fold in lightly with the vinegar.
5. Scoop the mixture into the circles and spread out to form two shells. An edging or low wall can be piped or shaped around the circumference of the shells.
6. Bake at 270° F for about 1¼ hours, until light and dry. If not quite dry, turn the oven off and leave the pavlova shells in the oven to cool overnight.
7. When cold, store in an airtight container in a cool place, until needed.

8. Assemble the pavlova just before serving, as the meringue softens when it comes into contact with moisture. Either top each shell/nest with ice cream, cream and fruit, or sandwich these ingredients between the two shells and garnish the top shell with whipped cream and strawberries.

Notes

Individual mini pavlovas can be made. Apart from being very attractive, these are easier to serve.

For a decadent variation, top the pavlova with scoops of caramel and ice cream (page 126) and chunks of halva. Drizzle with chocolate sauce (page 126).

Ice cream

10-12 servings

6 egg whites (see Notes)
pinch of salt
1 pint (2 cups) heavy cream
1 14-ounce can full cream sweetened condensed milk
2 teaspoons vanilla extract

1. Beat the egg whites with the salt until stiff but not dry.
2. Whip the cream until stiff and mix in the condensed milk and vanilla.
3. Fold in the egg whites.
4. Scoop into a large shallow container, cover and freeze overnight.

Notes

As a precaution, pasteurized liquid egg whites can be used in this recipe.

When beating the egg whites, the beater must be free of any traces of fat or oil. Any cream or yolk on the beater will prevent the whites from beating stiff. If fresh eggs are used, the yolks can be used to make baked custard (page 120).

Bar-One chocolate sauce

Yield: ¾ cup

MilkyWay bars, cut into pieces
1 tablespoon milk, half & half, or cream per 1.84 ounces of chocolate

1. Combine chocolate pieces and liquid in a pyrex jug.
2. Microwave at 50% power until melted, stirring at short intervals until smooth. Adjust the consistency by adding a little more liquid if necessary. Serve hot over ice cream.

Egg-free ice cream

10-12 servings

1 cup heavy cream
1 12-ounce can evaporated milk, chilled
1 14-ounce can full cream sweetened condensed milk
½ teaspoon vanilla extract
pinch of salt

1. Beat the cream until stiff.
2. Beat the evaporated milk until very stiff.
3. Fold the condensed milk, vanilla and salt into the evaporated milk.
4. Fold in the cream.
5. Scoop into a large, shallow container. Cover and freeze overnight.

Jelly whip-whip

6 servings

1 3-ounce package flavored jello
½ cup boiling water
1 12-ounce can evaporated milk, well chilled

1. Combine the jello and water in a saucepan and stir until the jello has dissolved.
2. Remove from the stove and set aside.
3. Beat the evaporated milk until stiff and doubled in volume.
4. Whisk the cooling jello for 1-2 minutes.
5. Gradually add the jello to the whipped evaporated milk while beating.
6. Refrigerate for 4-6 hours, until set.

Malvapoeding

*Although malvapoeding literally means "geranium pudding"
or "mallow pudding", this popular traditional dessert of Dutch
origin does not contain geraniums or mallows. One hypothesis is
that this dessert was named after a dessert wine, Malvasia, which
may have been served with the pudding during colonial times.*

6-8 servings

1 cup milk
1 tablespoon butter
1 tablespoon apricot jam   **Sauce**
1 egg   1 cup whipping or heavy
½ cup sugar   cream
1 tablespoon red wine vinegar   ½ cup milk
1 cup flour   6 tablespoons butter
1 teaspoon baking soda   ½ cup sugar

1. Heat the milk, butter and jam in a jug or saucepan until
   the butter has melted. Set aside.
2. Beat the egg and sugar together in a bowl until light and
   fluffy.
3. Add the vinegar to the milk mixture and fold it into the
   egg mixture together with the flour and baking soda.
4. Scoop into a greased 9-inch pie dish and bake at 350° F
   for 30-45 minutes, until a skewer inserted into the center
   comes out quite clean
5. Just before the pudding is ready, combine the sauce ingredients in a small saucepan and heat to boiling point,
   while stirring. Simmer for 3 minutes.
6. Remove the baked pudding from the oven and cut it
   into squares. Slowly pour the hot sauce over the pudding
   so that it is absorbed. Serve at room temperature with
   whipped cream.

Sticky date pudding

6-8 servings

½ pound pitted dates, chopped
1 teaspoon baking soda
1 cup boiling water

4 tablespoons (½ stick) butter or margarine
¼ cup brown sugar

2 eggs
1 cup flour
1 teaspoon baking powder

Toffee sauce
½ cup brown sugar
½ cup heavy cream
1 teaspoon vanilla extract
1 tablespoon butter or margarine

1. Mix the dates, baking soda and water together in a small bowl. Set aside.
2. Beat the butter and ¼ cup of sugar in a bowl until light and fluffy.
3. Add the eggs, one at a time, beating well after each addition.
4. Sift the flour and baking powder and fold it into the egg mixture.
5. Stir in the date mixture, and scoop into a greased 9-inch pie dish.
6. Bake at 350° F for 30-40 minutes, until a skewer inserted into center comes out quite clean.
7. While the pudding is baking, prepare the toffee sauce. Place all the sauce ingredients in a small saucepan and heat to boiling point while stirring.
8. Simmer for about 5 minutes, stirring occasionally.
9. Remove the baked pudding from the oven.
10. Loosen the edges with a knife and cut the pudding into portions. Top with the hot sauce. Serve with ice cream (page 126, page 127).

Notes

Consider doubling up the toffee sauce so that there is extra for serving with the dessert. This sauce also makes a great topping for ice cream.

Old Cape brandy pudding

A traditional favorite from the Cape, also known as Tipsy tart.

6-8 servings

½ pound pitted dates, sliced
1 teaspoon baking soda
1 cup boiling water

8 tablespoons (1 stick) butter
½ cup sugar
2 eggs
2 cups flour
1 teaspoon baking powder

pinch of salt
1 cup pecan or walnut pieces

Syrup
¾ cup water
2 tablespoons (¼ stick) butter
¾ cup sugar
1 teaspoon vanilla extract
¾ cup brandy

1. Put the dates into a small bowl and sprinkle with baking soda. Add the boiling water, mix and set aside to cool.
2. Cream the butter and sugar.
3. Add the eggs and beat well.
4. Add the date mixture and fold in the sifted dry ingredients, together with the nuts.
5. Scoop into a greased ovenproof dish and bake at 350° F for about 50 minutes, until a skewer inserted into the center comes out quite clean.
6. Make the syrup just before the pudding is ready. Heat the water, butter and sugar in a small saucepan, while stirring, until the sugar dissolves.
7. Boil rapidly for three minutes.
8. Remove from the heat and add the vanilla and brandy. Return to the stove and heat to boiling point just before using.
9. When the pudding is removed from the oven, cut it into portions and slowly pour the hot syrup over the pudding so that it is absorbed. Serve at room temperature with cream.

Jam roly-poly

6-8 servings

2 cups flour
2 teaspoons baking powder
pinch of salt
4 tablespoons (½ stick) butter
1 egg, whisked
½ cup cold water

½ cup apricot jam, slightly warmed

Syrup
1½ cups sugar
2 tablespoons (¼ stick) butter
½ teaspoon ground ginger
2½ cups water

1. Sift the flour, baking powder and salt together into a mixing bowl.
2. Rub in the 4 tablespoons of butter.
3. Cut in the egg and as much water as needed to form a workable dough.
4. Cover and set aside to rest for 15 minutes.
5. Roll the dough out on a lightly floured surface, to form a rectangle of about ¼ inch thick.
6. Spread lightly, or dot, with jam, keeping a jam-free zone around the edges.
7. Lightly roll up the dough from one of the short sides. Pinch the ends together.
8. Place in a narrow, lightly greased baking dish with the seam side down. The roll will lose its shape if baked in a large casserole dish.
9. Heat the syrup ingredients in a saucepan to boiling point, while stirring, to dissolve the sugar.
10. Pour the hot syrup over the roll.
11. Bake at 350° F for 50-60 minutes. Slice and serve with custard, cream or ice cream (page 126, page 127).

Notes
An attractive and easy variation is to cut the roll into 1½ inch slices and arrange them flat, jam edges showing, on the base of a greased casserole dish. Top with syrup and bake at 350° F for about 45 minutes.

Pannekoek

Pancakes - substantial crêpes.

Yield: 6-8

1 cup flour
¼ teaspoon baking powder
pinch of salt
1 egg
1 teaspoon vinegar
1 cup water
¼ cup oil

½ teaspoon ground cinnamon, mixed into
¼ cup sugar

orange and/or lemon wedges

1. Place the flour, baking powder and salt in a bowl.
2. Whisk the egg, vinegar, water and oil together.
3. Slowly add the liquid to the dry ingredients, while whisking, to form a smooth batter.
4. Set aside for at least an hour before making the pancakes.
5. Pour a thin layer of batter into a hot pan, greased with a little oil for the first pancake only. Brown lightly on both sides.
6. Stack the pancakes on a heated platter and keep warm until all the pancakes are made.
7. Sprinkle each pancake liberally with cinnamon-sugar before rolling up and serving with a wedge of fresh orange and/or lemon.

Buttermilk pudding

Traditional baked dessert.

6 servings

2 tablespoons (¼ stick) butter
⅔ cup sugar
3 eggs
1 cup flour
1 teaspoon baking powder
pinch of salt
1 cup milk
3 cups buttermilk

ground nutmeg or cinnamon

1. Cream the butter and sugar in a bowl.
2. Add the eggs and beat until smooth.
3. Fold in the sifted dry ingredients with the milk.
4. Mix in the buttermilk.
5. Pour into a large, greased, ovenproof bowl and sprinkle with a little nutmeg.
6. Place the bowl in a water bath (large Pyrex dish or deep baking pan containing 1-2 inches of warm water) and bake at 350° F for 50-60 minutes, until set. Serve hot, with ice cream (page 126, page 127) and/or warm honey mixed with cream.

Notes
Buttermilk pudding can be baked in the oven as above, but without using a water bath. The dessert will then draw a little water.

Japie se gunstelling

Little Jake's favorite; an orange-flavored, custard-like base with a slightly crusty topping.

4 servings

2 eggs, separated
½ cup sugar
1 cup milk
¼ cup flour
pinch of salt
1 cup freshly squeezed orange juice
1 tablespoon freshly squeezed lemon juice
zest of 1 orange
2 tablespoons (¼ stick) butter, melted

1. Beat the egg whites in a bowl, until stiff but not dry. Set aside.
2. Beat the sugar and egg yolks in a mixing bowl while slowly adding the milk.
3. Fold in the flour and salt.
4. Mix in the juices, zest and butter.
5. Fold in the stiffly beaten egg white.
6. Pour into a medium-sized, greased, ovenproof bowl.
7. Place the bowl in a water-bath (large Pyrex dish or deep baking pan containing 1-2 inches of warm water) and bake at 350° F for about 45 minutes, until set and lightly browned on top. Serve hot or cold with ice cream (page 126).

Notes

This pudding can be baked in the oven as above, but without using a water bath. The dessert will then draw a little water.

Ouma Cruywagen poeding

Nana Cruywagen pudding. Baked custard-like dessert.

4 servings

2 cups milk
1 cinnamon stick
2 eggs
3 tablespoons sugar
2 tablespoons flour
¼ teaspoon salt
1 tablespoon butter, cut into little pieces
ground nutmeg or cinnamon

1. Heat the milk with the cinnamon stick to boiling point in a saucepan.
2. Whisk the eggs and sugar in a mixing bowl.
3. Fold in the flour and salt.
4. Remove the cinnamon stick and pour the hot milk over the egg mixture, stirring all the time.
5. Pour into a greased baking dish, dot with butter and sprinkle with a little nutmeg.
6. Place the bowl in a water-bath (large Pyrex dish or deep baking pan containing 1-2 inches of warm water) and bake at 350° F for about 30 minutes, until set. Serve hot with berry jam or golden syrup (page 11).

Notes

This pudding can be baked in the oven as above, but without using a water bath. The dessert will then draw a little water.

Peach crumble

4-6 servings

1 15.25-ounce can yellow
cling peach slices, drained
and cut into bite-sized pieces
1 cup old fashioned rolled oats
⅔ cup crunchy brown sugar

1 cup flour
1 teaspoon ground cinnamon
pinch of salt
8 tablespoons (1 stick) butter,
room temperature

1. Arrange the peaches in a greased pie dish.
2. Put all the dry ingredients into a mixing bowl.
3. Mix in the butter, to form a loose, crumbly topping.
4. Sprinkle the topping over the peaches.
5. Bake at 350° F for 30 minutes, or until lightly browned. Serve
   with whipped cream or ice cream (page 126, page 127).

Fruit cocktail tart

8-10 servings

2 eggs
¾ cup sugar
2 cups flour
1 tablespoon baking powder
¼ teaspoon salt
1 teaspoon baking soda
1 15-ounce can fruit cocktail
in natural fruit juice

Sauce
⅔ cup sugar
1 teaspoon vanilla extract
¾ cup evaporated milk
1 tablespoon butter
1 cup shredded coconut,
unsweetened

1. Beat the eggs and 1 cup of sugar in a mixing bowl until
   light and fluffy.
2. Fold in the flour, baking powder, salt, baking soda and
   fruit cocktail with juice.

3. Scoop into a large, greased, baking dish and bake at 350° F for 30–45 minutes.
4. Mix the sauce ingredients in a small saucepan and bring to the boil, while stirring.
5. Lower the temperature and leave to simmer for 5–10 minutes.
6. When ready, remove the tart from the oven, loosen the edges and cut into squares.
7. Pour the hot sauce over the tart. Serve at room temperature.

Saucepan pudding

Cake-like dumplings in a gingery sauce.

8-10 servings

	8 tablespoons (1 stick) butter
2½ cups water	½ cup apricot jam
1 cup sugar	2 teaspoons baking soda
pinch of salt	1½ cups flour
1 teaspoon ground ginger	pinch of salt

1. Heat the first four ingredients to boiling point in a medium to large saucepan, while stirring. Once the sugar has dissolved, lower the temperature and leave the syrup to simmer.
2. In another saucepan, melt the butter with the jam.
3. Stir in the baking soda.
4. Lower the temperature and mix in the flour and salt. Keep stirring until the dough leaves the sides of the saucepan and forms a ball.
5. Drop spoonfuls of this mixture into the syrup. Adjust the temperature so that the syrup continues to simmer.
6. Cover the saucepan with a lid and simmer for 20 minutes. Serve hot with custard, cream or ice cream (page 126, page 127).

Souskluitjies

Saucy dumplings.

6-8 servings

1 cup sugar
pinch of cream of tartar
5 cups water
1 cup flour
1 ½ teaspoons baking powder
pinch of salt

2 tablespoons sugar
2 tablespoons (¼ stick) butter
1 egg
⅓ cup milk
¼ cup dried tart cherries,
cranberries or raisins
¼ cup pecan nuts coarsely
chopped

1. Combine the 1 cup of sugar, cream of tartar and about ¼ cup of the water in a large saucepan.
2. Stir over medium heat until the sugar has dissolved. Increase the temperature and boil rapidly without stirring, until the syrup becomes light brown in color. (A drop of the syrup will form a hard ball in a saucer of cold water).
3. Remove the saucepan from the heat and carefully stir in the remaining water.
4. Return to the stove and bring to the boil. Leave to simmer while making the dumplings.
5. Sift the dry ingredients into a mixing bowl and rub in the butter.
6. Whisk the egg and milk in a cup and cut into the flour mixture, together with the fruit and nuts.
7. Drop small spoonfuls of the batter into the boiling syrup.
8. Cover with a lid and simmer for 15-20 minutes, until cooked through. Serve with custard, whipped cream or ice cream (page 126, page 127).

Telephone pudding

A party line, or shared telephone service, was common during the first half of the 20th century. Two or more subscribers were connected to the same service loop. In rural areas, where population density was sparse, these loops were quite extensive. Each subscriber had a distinctive ring and calls were made through an operator. When the line was in service, no other calls could be made, although this did not deter subscribers from listening in on each others' conversations; a boon for local gossips. Lore has it that this easy recipe was originally given by one friend to another over the telephone, and was then spread far and wide by the eavesdroppers.

6-8 servings

1 cup sugar
2½ cups boiling water
1 teaspoon vanilla extract

8 tablespoons (1 stick) butter or margarine

¾ cup sugar
1 egg
1 teaspoon baking soda
1 cup milk
1½ cups flour
pinch of salt
1 teaspoon ground ginger
2 tablespoons apricot jam

1. Mix 1 cup of sugar with the boiling water and vanilla in a large ovenproof bowl (capacity of at least 1 quart) and stir until the sugar dissolves. Set aside.
2. Cream the butter and remaining sugar in a mixing bowl.
3. Whisk the egg into the mixture.
4. Stir the baking soda into the milk.
5. Sift the dry ingredients and add, alternately with the milk, to the batter.
6. Add the jam and mix lightly.
7. Scoop the batter into the sauce.
8. Bake at 350° F for 30-45 minutes. Serve with custard, whipped cream or ice cream (page 126, page 127).

Vinegar pudding

Cake-like pudding in a sauce, containing only basic ingredients that one is likely to have in stock.

6-8 servings

2 cups water
1½ cups sugar
¼ cup vinegar

2 tablespoons (¼ stick) butter or margarine
½ cup sugar
2 eggs
1½ cups flour
1 teaspoon baking soda
2 teaspoons ground ginger
½ teaspoon ground nutmeg
¼ teaspoon salt
2 tablespoons apricot jam

1. Put the water, 1½ cups of sugar and vinegar into a saucepan. Bring to the boil, stirring until the sugar dissolves, and leave to simmer for 5 minutes.
2. Pour the sauce into a large casserole dish and set aside to cool slightly.
3. Cream the butter and remaining ½ cup of sugar in a mixing bowl.
4. Add the eggs, one at a time, beating well after each addition.
5. Mix the sifted dry ingredients and the jam into the butter-egg mixture.
6. Scoop the batter into the sauce.
7. Bake at 350° F for 30-40 minutes. Serve with custard or cream.

Pumpkin fritters

Traditionally served as a dessert with cinnamon-sugar.

Yield: 10-12

2 cups cooked, mashed pumpkin or butternut, chilled or at
room temperature
½ cup flour
¾ teaspoon baking powder
pinch of salt
1 egg, whisked
water or milk as needed

oil for frying

¼ cup sugar, mixed with
½ teaspoon ground cinnamon

1. Combine the pumpkin, flour, baking powder, and salt in a
   mixing bowl.
2. Add the egg and mix well.
3. The batter should be of a dropping consistency. If it is
   too stiff, add a little water or milk; if it is too runny, add
   a little more flour.
4. Heat enough oil in a frying pan to shallow-fry the fritters.
5. Drop spoonfuls of the batter into the oil.
6. Fry until lightly browned on both sides.
7. Drain on paper toweling and sprinkle with cinnamon-
   sugar. Serve hot.

Steamed Christmas pudding

6-8 servings

2 ounces dried cranberries
2 ounces dried tart cherries, halved
1 ounce dates, chopped
2 ounces golden raisins
1 ounce seedless raisins
¼ cup brandy or orange juice mixed with ½ cup water
4 tablespoons (½ stick) butter or margarine
⅓ cup sugar
½ teaspoon baking soda
⅔ cup flour
¼ teaspoon salt
1 teaspoon baking powder
1 teaspoon ground allspice
½ teaspoon ground nutmeg
¼ teaspoon ground ginger
⅓ cup fresh white breadcrumbs
2 tablespoons marmalade
1 egg, whisked

1. Place the fruit, liquid, butter and sugar in a saucepan and bring to the boil, while stirring.
2. Cover and simmer for 5 minutes. Stir in the baking soda and set aside to cool for 15-20 minutes.
3. Mix the flour, salt, baking powder, allspice, nutmeg and ginger in a mixing bowl.
4. Add the fruit mixture, together with the breadcrumbs, marmalade and egg.
5. Mix lightly and scoop into a greased pudding bowl, 2½ pint (5 cup) capacity. The bowl should not be more than ⅔ full.
6. Cover with a lid or parchment paper and foil. Mold the foil securely round the top of the bowl to seal.
7. Place the bowl in a steamer or in a saucepan on a thick wad of paper toweling or an inverted saucer, so that the bowl is not in direct contact with the heat of the saucepan base.
8. Add boiling water to reach about halfway up the side of the bowl.

9. Cover with a lid and boil for 1½ hours. Replenish water if necessary.
10. Using oven gloves, carefully take the bowl out of the steamer. Remove the cover, loosen the dessert with a knife and tip it out onto a heated platter. Serve with brandy butter.

Notes

If made ahead of time, leave the pudding in the bowl and store in a cool, dry place until needed.

To re-heat, steam for 40-50 minutes, or microwave at 50% power for 10 minutes.

If available, an 8-ounce packet of fruit cake mix can replace the dried fruits listed above. Traditionally, cranberries and tart cherries would not have been used, but they add a pleasant local flavor to this dessert.

Brandy butter

The finishing touch for the Christmas pudding.

8 tablespoons (1 stick) butter
¼ cup confectioners powder sugar
3 tablespoons brandy

1. Cream the butter and sugar until light and fluffy.
2. Add the brandy and mix until blended.
3. Cover and refrigerate until needed. Serve cold.

Cremora log

A variation of a popular fridge tart.

8 ounces (2¼ cups) powdered coffee creamer
1 cup boiling water
1 14-ounce can sweetened condensed milk
¼ cup lemon juice
½ cup sliced or diced strawberries, optional
12 rectangular graham crackers
large piece of heavy-duty aluminum foil,
approximately 12 x 15 inches

whipped cream
mint crisp chocolate, melted
fresh fruit

1. Measure the coffee creamer into a bowl and gradually add the boiling water, while mixing with a whisk to form a smooth milky liquid.
2. Set aside to cool for at least an hour.
3. Add the condensed milk and lemon juice to the milky liquid, while whisking. The mixture will thicken. Refrigerate for 1-2 hours, until partially set.
4. Arrange six crackers on the foil (two rows of three crackers each). This will give you a rectangle of approximately 7x10 inches.
5. Spread half of the filling over this base.
6. Place the remaining six crackers on top and cover with the rest of the filling. If using fruit, arrange it down the center of the middle crackers.
7. Carefully lift the long sides of the foil and bring them together to form the top of a triangle.

8. Fold the long edges of the foil together securely and shape the log into a smooth triangle by running your hands along the sides.
9. Seal the two short sides and refrigerate overnight or freeze for a few hours.
10. Carefully remove the foil and smooth the sides of the triangle with a spatula.
11. Cover with cream, drizzle chocolate over the tart and decorate with fruit.

Crêpes Suzette

6-8 servings

1 cup flour
pinch of salt
2 eggs
1 cup water
2 teaspoons brandy
1 tablespoon butter, melted

¼ cup apricot jam
¼ cup marmalade

Sauce
¾ cup sugar
¾ cup cream
2 tablespoons brandy
2 tablespoons lemon juice
2 cups freshly squeezed orange juice
1 teaspoon lemon zest
2 teaspoons orange zest
½ teaspoon ground ginger
pinch of salt

1. Place the flour and salt in a bowl.
2. Whisk the eggs with the water and add to the dry ingredients, mixing to form a smooth batter.
3. Stir in the brandy and set aside for at least 2 hours.
4. Stir in the butter just before making the crêpes.
5. Pour a thin layer of batter into a hot crêpe pan, greased with a little oil for the first crêpe only. Brown lightly on both sides.
6. When all the crêpes are made, mix the jam and marmalade together and spoon a little onto each crêpe before folding into quarters and arranging in an attractive casserole dish.
7. Put the sauce ingredients into a saucepan and heat to boiling point, while stirring to dissolve the sugar.
8. Pour the hot sauce over the crêpes, cover with a lid or foil, and set aside for at least 30 minutes. Serve hot with ice cream (page 126, page 127).

Notes

These Crêpes Suzette freeze well. Thaw and heat through in the oven at 350° F for 20-30 minutes, or in the microwave, before serving.

Hertzoggies

Honey tea cake

Guava cheese fridge tart

Brandy snaps

Dadelgoedjies

Teatime Treats

Melktert

Milk tart, a traditional custard tart flavored with cinnamon.

Yield: 1 9-inch tart

Filling
2+½ cups milk
1 cinnamon stick
¼ cup sugar
3 tablespoons flour
2 tablespoons cornstarch
pinch of salt
2 tablespoons (¼ stick) butter
3 eggs, separated
½ teaspoon vanilla extract

1 sheet prepared puff pastry, thawed

dash of ground cinnamon mixed with
1 tablespoon sugar

1. Place 2 cups of milk and the cinnamon stick in a heavy-based saucepan, and heat to just below boiling point.
2. Combine the sugar, flour, cornstarch and salt in a mixing bowl. While stirring, gradually add the remaining ½ cup of milk to form a smooth paste.
3. Stir the hot milk into the flour mixture and then return this mix to the saucepan. Stir over low heat until thick and smooth.
4. Remove from the stove and mix in the butter. Set aside to cool for 30-45 minutes.
5. While the custard is cooling, line a lightly greased, deep pie dish with the pastry. Use cut-offs of pastry for a second layer around the rim. Seal together with cold water. Prick the base and set it aside in a cool place until needed.
6. When the custard is cool, remove the cinnamon stick and beat in the egg yolks, one at a time.
7. Add the vanilla.
8. Beat the egg whites to the soft-peak stage (i.e., foamy but not dry) and fold thoroughly into the custard.
9. Pour the filling into the prepared base and bake at 400° F for 10 minutes.
10. Lower the oven temperature to 350° F and bake for a further 20-25 minutes, until the filling has set. Sprinkle with cinnamon-sugar before serving warm or cold.

Apple almond teacake

6-8 servings

¾ cup (1½ sticks) butter or margarine, room temperature
1 cup sugar
3 eggs
1½ cups flour
2 teaspoons baking powder
pinch of salt
½ cup milk
1½ cups shredded coconut, unsweetened
2 medium-large cooking apples (e.g., Granny Smith), peeled, cored and diced

½ cup sliced almonds
2 tablespoons crunchy brown sugar

1. Cream the butter and sugar until light and fluffy.
2. Add the eggs, one at a time, beating after each addition.
3. Sift in the flour, baking powder and salt, and mix in the milk.
4. Fold in the coconut and apple.
5. Scoop into a greased baking dish or pan. Sprinkle almonds and brown sugar over the top.
6. Bake at 350° F for 50-60 minutes. Cut into squares and serve with whipped cream.

Honey teacake

4-6 servings

½ cup milk
3 tablespoons butter
1 egg
½ cup sugar
1 cup flour
1 ½ teaspoons baking powder
pinch of salt

Sauce
4 tablespoons (½ stick) butter
2 tablespoons honey

1. Heat the milk with the 3 tablespoons of butter in a small saucepan or jug until the butter has melted.
2. Beat the egg and sugar in a mixing bowl until pale and fluffy.
3. Sift the flour, baking powder and salt over the sugar mixture, and fold in lightly with the buttery milk mixture. Do not overmix.
4. Scrape into a greased 9-inch pie dish and bake at 350 °F for 25-30 minutes, until cooked.
5. Meanwhile, make the sauce by heating ½ stick of butter with the honey, until the butter melts.
6. When the cake is ready, remove it from the oven and cut it into serving-sized portions. Pour the sauce over the cake; it will soak into the cake. Serve hot or cold with cream.

Swiss roll

Also known as jam roll, jelly roll or sponge roll.

6-8 servings

3 eggs, separated
½ cup sugar
1 tablespoon lemon juice
½ cup flour
1 teaspoon baking powder

½ cup strawberry or apricot jam, slightly warmed
sugar

1. Line a Swiss roll pan (12x8 or 13x9 inches) with parchment paper. Set aside.
2. Beat the egg whites until foamy. Gradually add 1 tablespoon of the sugar and whip until stiff. Set aside.
3. Beat the egg yolks with the remaining sugar and the lemon juice until thick and pale in color.
4. Sift the flour and baking powder and fold into the yolk mixture.
5. Add the egg white and fold in lightly.
6. Spoon the mixture into the prepared pan and spread to cover the surface.
7. Bake at 400° F for 10–12 minutes. Test by pressing the sponge gently but firmly with a finger. If no impression is left, it is ready to be removed from the oven.
8. Turn out onto a damp dishcloth and carefully remove the parchment paper.
9. Spread with jam and roll up carefully, from one of the short sides, using the cloth to support the sponge as it is rolled. Using a sharp knife, cut off the dry edges (about ¼ inch on either side).
10. Leave covered for 10 minutes before transferring to a cooling rack. Sprinkle with a little sugar.

Guava-cheese fridge tart

Yield: 1 9-inch tart

½ Swiss roll, thinly sliced
2 teaspoons gelatin
3 tablespoons cold water
¼ cup custard powder (page 10)
½ cup cold water
1 15-ounce can guava halves in heavy syrup (page 11),
drained and cut into small pieces, syrup retained
1 8-ounce package low fat cream cheese, room temperature
½ 14-ounce can full cream sweetened condensed milk
¼ cup lemon juice

1. Line the base of a 9-inch pie plate with slices of Swiss roll.
2. Sprinkle the gelatin over 3 tablespoons of water, in a small
    bowl. Let it stand for a minute. Leave to clarify over a
    bowl or saucepan of boiling hot water.
3. Mix the custard powder, ½ cup water and the syrup
    (from the guavas) in a small saucepan. Stir over medium
    heat until it becomes very thick.
4. Fold in the guava pieces and set aside to cool.
5. Beat the cream cheese, condensed milk and lemon juice in
    a mixing bowl until smooth. Mix in the gelatin.
6. Spread the cream cheese mixture over the cake base.
7. Spoon the guava-custard mixture over the cream cheese
    layer.
8. Refrigerate for a few hours before serving.

Notes

If guavas are not obtainable, this tart can be made with
pear halves in heavy syrup. Alternatively, an 8-ounce can
of crushed pineapple can be added, with its juice, to the
custard powder and water.

Leftover condensed milk can be added to coffee instead
of milk and sugar or eaten as is!

Caramel-mint fridge tart

8-10 servings

1 pint heavy whipping cream
1 14-ounce can caramel (dulce de leche)
1 7.2-ounce packet Graham crackers, approximately
1 3-ounce slab milk chocolate with mint crisps, grated

1. Pour the cream into a large mixing bowl and beat until stiff.
2. Spread caramel on top of 6-8 crackers and arrange in a dish to cover the base.
3. Cover with a layer of cream.
4. Sprinkle some chocolate over the cream.
5. Top with another layer of biscuits, spread with caramel.
6. Repeat the layers, ending with a layer of cream, sprinkled with the last bit of chocolate.
7. Cover and refrigerate.

Notes

Replace Graham crackers with Tennis biscuits (page 11), if available.

Plain milk chocolate, grated and mixed with crushed peppermint candy, can be used instead of milk chocolate with mint crisps.

Dulce de leche can sometimes be found in the Spanish food section of stores.

Sponge loaf

Yield: 1 small loaf

3 eggs
½ cup sugar

½ teaspoon vanilla extract
½ cup flour, sifted
pinch of salt

1. Whisk the eggs very well until thick and pale in color.
2. Add the sugar in thirds, beating well after each addition. Add the vanilla.
3. Lightly fold in the flour and salt, in thirds.
4. Scoop into a lined loaf tin.
5. Bake at 350° F for 40 minutes, until cooked. Leave the cake in the tin for a few minutes and then turn it out carefully to cool on a cooling rack.

Coconut macaroons

Yield: 4 dozen

1 14-ounce can full cream sweetened condensed milk
6 cups shredded coconut, unsweetened

2 teaspoons vanilla extract
4 egg whites
pinch of salt
dried cranberries or cherries

1. Mix the condensed milk, coconut and vanilla together in a large bowl.
2. Whisk the egg whites with the salt until stiff but not dry (soft-peak stage) and fold into the coconut mixture.
3. Spoon walnut-sized portions onto lined or greased baking trays.
4. Top each macaroon with a piece of cranberry.
5. Bake at 275° F for about 30 minutes. Turn the oven off and leave the macaroons in the oven for a further 20-30 minutes, until they are light brown in color. Macaroons will harden as they cool.

Koeksisters

Traditional braided, doughnut-like treat drenched in syrup.

Yield: 24

Syrup
4 cups sugar
2 cups water
½ teaspoon ground ginger
pinch of salt
2 cinnamon sticks

The syrup should be made first and chilled, preferably overnight. The hot, drained koeksisters must be submerged in icy cold syrup.

Dough
4 cups flour
½ teaspoon salt
4 teaspoons baking powder
6 tablespoons (¾ stick) butter, room temperature
2 eggs, beaten
2 tablespoons lemon juice mixed with
⅔ cup cold water

4-6 cups oil

1. Make the syrup a day in advance. Mix all the ingredients together in a saucepan and heat to boiling point, stirring gently so that the sugar dissolves.
2. Reduce the heat and leave to simmer for 5 minutes.
3. Remove from the heat and chill.
4. Refrigerate overnight.
5. Make the dough 12-24 hours later, as follows. Combine the flour, salt and baking powder in a bowl and rub in the butter.
6. Mix in the egg and cut in the liquid to form the dough.
7. Knead for a couple of minutes to develop elasticity. Cover and set aside for at least an hour.

8. On a lightly floured surface, roll out the dough to form a rectangle of about ¼ inch thick.
9. Cut the dough into strips of about 2½ inches wide.
10. Cut across the strips at 2-inch intervals, to create 2½x2-inch oblongs.
11. Make two partial cuts into each 2½x2-inch oblong. This will result in three mini strips for braiding.
12. At this point, divide the syrup between two bowls and leave them in the freezer while braiding the dough.
13. Braid the dough. Pinch the top together and braid the three mini strips loosely. Then pinch the loose ends together at the bottom. Set aside in a cool place until all the dough is braided.
14. Heat the oil in a fryer or deep saucepan, to 365° F (see Notes).
15. Deep-fry about 5 koeksisters at a time, for 1-2 minutes, until lightly browned.
16. Remove one bowl of syrup from the freezer.
17. Using a perforated spoon or spider skimmer, transfer the koeksisters from the hot oil directly to the cold syrup.
18. Submerge the hot koeksisters in the icy cold syrup for about 30 seconds.
19. Arrange on cooling racks over greaseproof paper (to catch up the excess syrup).
20. Return the bowl of syrup to the freezer and use the other, colder bowl for the next batch.

Notes

The oil will have reached 365° F when a 1-inch square of day-old bread, dropped into the oil, takes about 1 minute to brown.

Koeksisters freeze well.

Scones

Yield: 8-10

2 cups flour
3½ teaspoons baking powder
¼ teaspoon salt
2 tablespoons sugar (optional)
4 tablespoons (½ stick) butter, cold
1 egg
water, icy cold

1. Sift the dry ingredients into a bowl. Cut the butter into pieces and rub the pieces lightly into the dry ingredients using your fingertips.
2. Break the egg into a measuring jug and add water to a volume of ¾ cup.
3. Whisk the egg and water and cut this mixture into the dry ingredients, until the liquid is just incorporated. Do not overmix. A little more or less liquid may be needed, depending on the moisture content of the flour.
4. Pat out gently on a lightly floured surface to a thickness of about 2 inches. Cut scones with a cookie cutter or wine glass, dipped in flour before each scone is cut.
5. Pack the scones snugly together on a lined or greased baking sheet.
6. Bake at 400° F for 12-18 minutes, until cooked. Serve with whipped cream or grated cheese and an assortment of jams.

Notes

For best results, ingredients should be as cold as possible and should not be overmixed.

For savory scones, omit the sugar and add a pinch of salt, a pinch of cayenne pepper and ¼ teaspoon ground mustard. For cheese scones, add ½ cup grated cheese to the savory scone mix.

Oil-based scones

Yield: 6-8

¼ cup oil
1 egg
½ cup milk, approximately
2 cups flour
1 tablespoon baking powder
¼ teaspoon salt

1. Place the oil and egg in a measuring jug. Add milk to a volume of 1 cup and whisk together well.
2. Sift the flour, baking powder, and salt into mixing bowl.
3. Using a knife or spatula, cut the liquid into the flour. Work quickly and lightly; do not overmix.
4. On a lightly floured surface, shape the dough into a round of about 2 inches thick.
5. Cut scones with a cookie cutter or wine glass, dipped in flour before each scone is cut.
6. Pack the scones snugly together on a lined or greased baking sheet.
7. Bake at 400° F for 12-18 minutes, until lightly browned and baked through. Serve with whipped cream or grated cheese and an assortment of jams.

Notes

Instead of cutting individual scones, the round of dough can be lightly cut into wedges, and the wedges separated after baking.

For a savory variation, bake the dough as a round, in a pie plate, at 400° F for 10 minutes. Melt 2 tablespoons of butter with 1 teaspoon of Marmite (page 11) in a cup, and pour over the par-baked round scone. Top with 1 cup of grated cheese and return to the oven for about 10 minutes, until done.

Drop scones

Yield: 6-8

2 cups flour
1 tablespoon baking powder
1 tablespoon sugar, optional
pinch of salt
4 tablespoons (½ stick) butter
1 egg
½ cup water
½ cup milk

1. Sift the dry ingredients into a mixing bowl and rub in the butter.
2. Whisk the egg, water and milk in a jug and cut lightly into the flour mixture.
3. Drop spoonfuls of dough onto a lined or greased baking sheet and bake at 400° F for 10-15 minutes, until cooked. Serve with whipped cream or grated cheese and an assortment of jams.

Notes

For savory cheese scones, omit the sugar. Add a pinch of cayenne pepper and ¼ teaspoon ground mustard to the dry ingredients. Use 3 tablespoons butter, instead of 4, and add ½ cup grated cheese to the butter-flour mixture.

Crumpets

Similar to American pancakes. Also known as flapjacks.

Yield: 16-20

1½ cups flour
2 teaspoons baking powder
pinch of salt
1 tablespoon sugar
2 eggs
2 tablespoons (¼ stick) butter, melted
1 cup milk

1. Sift the dry ingredients into a bowl.
2. Whisk the eggs and butter in a jug and add the milk.
3. Mix into the dry ingredients with a cutting motion. Do not overmix. The mixture should be a little lumpy.
4. Set the batter aside for at least an hour before using.
5. Drop spoonfuls of the batter onto a hot, lightly greased griddle or frying pan. The crumpets should be about ¼ inch thick and 2½-3 inches in diameter.
6. Cook over medium heat. Turn over once, when bubbles form on the surface. Serve with butter, honey or jam and cheese.

Notes

The pan/griddle need only be greased before cooking the first batch.

Drop the batter from the tip of the spoon for well-shaped crumpets.

Chocolate éclairs

Yield: 8-10

Choux pastry
8 tablespoons (1 stick) butter
or margarine
1 cup boiling water
1 cup flour
4 eggs

Filling
Crème patisserie or
1 cup heavy cream, stiffly
beaten with
1-2 tablespoons sugar
½ teaspoon vanilla extract

Chocolate glaze
3 ounces chocolate
2 tablespoons butter

1. Put the butter and boiling water into a saucepan and boil until the butter has melted. Add the flour and stir vigorously.
2. Cook over low heat, stirring continuously, until the mixture becomes a smooth, shiny ball.
3. Remove from the heat and set aside to cool for 5-10 minutes. Add the eggs, one at a time, beating after each addition with an electric hand beater. Beat until the dough becomes paste-like in appearance.
4. Spoon the choux paste into an icing bag (or a plastic bag with a corner cut off), with a wide, plain nozzle.
5. Squeeze the paste into segments of about 1 inch wide and 5 inches long, onto a lined or greased baking sheet. Allow space between the éclairs for expansion.
6. Bake at 400° F for 10 minutes. Reduce the temperature to 325° F and bake for a further 10-20 minutes, until lightly browned and set.
7. When the éclairs are cool, cut them horizontally with a sharp knife and fill them with the sweet filling.
8. Make the glaze by melting the chocolate and butter in a bowl, either over a saucepan of hot water or in the microwave.
9. Spread a thin layer of the chocolate glaze onto the filled éclairs using the back of a spoon or a small spatula.

Notes

Remove one éclair after 20 minutes of baking. The éclairs will be cooked if it keeps its shape and does not collapse.

Crème patisserie

Thick custard.

Yield: about 1 cup

1+¼ cup milk
2 egg yolks
3 tablespoons sugar
2 tablespoons flour
1 tablespoon cornstarch
pinch of salt
1 tablespoon butter
½ teaspoon vanilla extract

1. Heat 1 cup of milk in a saucepan to just below boiling point.
2. Whisk the remaining ¼ cup milk with the yolks.
3. Combine the sugar, flour, cornstarch and salt in a bowl. Gradually whisk in the milk-yolk mixture to form a smooth paste.
4. Add the hot milk, while stirring.
5. Return to the saucepan and stir over medium heat until the custard thickens.
6. Remove the custard from the stove and stir in the butter and vanilla. Set it aside to cool.

Choux pastry puffs

Yield: 30-40 small puffs

8 tablespoons (1 stick) butter or margarine
1 cup boiling water
1 cup flour
4 eggs

1. Put the butter and boiling water into a saucepan and boil until the butter has melted.
2. Reduce the heat. Add the flour and stir vigorously.
3. Cook over low heat, stirring continuously, until the mixture becomes a smooth, shiny ball.
4. Remove from the heat and set aside to cool for 5-10 minutes. Add the eggs, one at a time, beating after each addition with an electric hand beater. Beat until the dough becomes paste-like in appearance.
5. Drop teaspoonfuls onto a lined or greased baking sheet. Leave spaces between the puffs to allow for expansion.
6. Bake at 400° F for 10 minutes. Reduce the temperature to 325° F and bake for a further 10-20 minutes, until lightly browned and set.

Notes

Remove one puff after 20 minutes of baking. The puffs will be cooked if it keeps its shape and does not collapse.

Choux puffs can be filled with a variety of sweet fillings, such as:
- Fresh cream whipped with sugar to taste, and a few drops of vanilla extract.
- Whipped cream mixed with fresh or canned fruit.
- Crème patisserie, with or without fruit.
When filled, sprinkle with a little confectioners powder sugar.

Choux puffs can also be filled with savory fillings, such as:
- A blend of cream cheese and sour cream mixed with finely chopped green onion and chopped ham.
- Spinach and cheese filling.

Fruit Mince pies

Traditional Christmas fare.

Yield: 6-8

Short crust pastry
1 ½ cups flour
pinch of salt
8 tablespoons (1 stick) butter
¼ cup iced water, approximately

¾ cup fruit mince, approximately

sugar

1. Mix the flour, salt and butter in a bowl, until the mixture resembles fine breadcrumbs.
2. Add a little water and mix to form a soft dough.
3. Refrigerate for at least an hour before using.
4. Roll the pastry out thinly, to a thickness of approximately ⅛ inch.
5. Line small muffin pans or shallow patty pans with rounds of pastry.
6. Put a spoonful of fruit mince onto each pastry base and cover with a lid of pastry, sealing the edges together with a little cold water. Crimp or flute the edges.
7. Make a few incisions in the top of each pie with the point of a sharp knife for the steam to escape.
8. Bake at 400° F for 8 minutes and then reduce the temperature to 350° F and bake for a further 6-10 minutes.
9. When cold, sprinkle with sugar. Serve warm or at room temperature.

Notes
Fruit mince is sometimes stocked in the international aisle of grocery stores and in specialty stores. To make your own, see page 193.

Hertzoggies

Little jam tartlets topped with coconut. Supposedly a favorite of General Hertzog, who served as a Boer general during the second Anglo Boer war and as Prime Minister of the Union of South Africa from 1924 to 1939.

Yield: 48

8 tablespoons (1 stick) butter	¾ cup apricot jam, approximately
½ cup sugar	mately
pinch of salt	4 egg whites
2 egg yolks	¼ teaspoon cream of tartar
2 cups flour	¼ cup sugar
1 teaspoon baking powder	2 cups shredded coconut,
¼ cup milk	unsweetened

1. Cream the butter, sugar and salt in a bowl, until light and fluffy.
2. Add the yolks and beat well.
3. Mix in the flour, baking powder and milk to form a soft dough.
4. Knead lightly and shape into a ball.
5. Roll the dough out thinly, to a thickness of about ⅛ inch, and cut into small rounds with a cookie cutter or glass dipped in flour, to fit lightly greased, shallow patty pans or mini muffin pans.
6. Place half a teaspoon of jam in the center of each base.
7. Whisk the egg whites with the cream of tartar, until foamy. Slowly add the sugar and beat until stiff but not dry.
8. Lightly fold in the coconut and top each tartlet with a spoonful of this mixture.
9. Bake at 350° F for 15-20 minutes, until golden brown.

Notes
Use pasteurized egg whites for the two extra whites needed in the topping, or make a half quantity of baked custard (page 120) with the two remaining yolks if fresh eggs are used.

Jam cookies

Yield: 30

1 cup (2 sticks) butter or margarine, room temperature
⅔ cup sugar
1 egg
1 teaspoon vanilla extract
3 cups flour
2 teaspoons baking powder
pinch of salt
½ - ¾ cup apricot jam, slightly warmed

1. Cream the butter and sugar in a mixing bowl until light and fluffy.
2. Beat in the egg and vanilla.
3. Sift in the flour, baking powder and salt. Mix to form a soft dough.
4. Press ⅔ of the dough onto a greased and lightly floured baking sheet, to a thickness of about ¼ inch.
5. Spread a layer of jam over the base.
6. Coarsely grate the remaining dough over the jam layer.
7. Bake at 350° F for about 20 minutes, until lightly browned. Cool slightly before cutting into squares.

Brandy snaps

Yield: 16

¼ cup golden syrup (page 11)
4 tablespoons (½ stick) butter or margarine
¼ cup sugar
1 teaspoon lemon juice
½ cup flour
1 teaspoon ground ginger
pinch of salt

1. Heat the syrup, butter, sugar and lemon juice in a sauce-pan and simmer until the butter has melted.
2. Remove from the stove.
3. Add the remaining ingredients and mix well.
4. Drop teaspoonfuls onto a lined or greased baking sheet. Make only 3 or 4 at a time, leaving plenty of room for spreading.
5. Bake at 380° F for 5 minutes, until light brown.
6. Remove from the oven and cool for about a minute, until just cool enough to handle. Carefully lift each brandy snap with a spatula and wrap it around the handle of a wooden spoon to form a tube. Set it aside. Once firm, remove the snap from the handle and place it on a cooling rack. Should the snaps harden before being shaped, return them to the oven for a few seconds to soften. Store in an airtight container.

Notes

Fill with brandy-flavored, stiffly whipped cream shortly before serving. The snaps will soften when exposed to moisture.

Outydse soetkoekies

Old fashioned sweet cookies.

Yield: 60

2 cups flour
pinch of salt
1 teaspoon baking soda
¼ teaspoon ground cloves
1 teaspoon ground ginger
2 teaspoons ground cinnamon
1 cup sugar
zest of 1 orange
8 tablespoons (1 stick) butter, room temperature
1 egg
1-2 tablespoons water or sweet wine

1. Mix the dry ingredients together in a bowl or food processor.
2. Add the zest and blend in the butter.
3. Whisk the egg with 1 tablespoon of water and mix/blend into the butter mixture to form a soft dough.
4. Knead lightly and set aside for at least an hour before baking.
5. Cut off workable pieces of dough, roll each piece out to a thickness of about ¼ inch and cut into rounds of about 2 inches in diameter.
6. Arrange on greased or lined baking trays and bake at 400° F for about 10 minutes.

Chocolate fridge biscuits

Yield: 30-36

1 7.05-ounce packet Tennis (page 11) or Marie biscuits
1 cup (2 sticks) butter
4 cups confectioners powder sugar
2 egg whites (see Notes)
¼ cup unsweetened cocoa
½ teaspoon vanilla extract

1. Place the biscuits in a plastic bag, close the bag and crush the biscuits coarsely with a rolling pin.
2. Melt the butter and add the sugar.
3. Stir in the egg whites, cocoa and vanilla, and mix until smooth.
4. Gently mix in the biscuit pieces, until they are well coated.
5. Press the mixture into a baking pan or dish, lined with parchment paper.
6. Cover and refrigerate. Cut into fingers or blocks when cold.

Notes

Graham crackers or Maria biscuits (available in the Spanish section of some supermarkets) can be used instead of Tennis or Marie biscuits. Maria biscuits are very similar to Marie biscuits.

The eggs are not cooked in this recipe. As a precaution, pasteurized liquid egg whites can be used.

Dadelgoedjies

Little date things; crispy date balls covered with coconut.

Yield: 20

½ pound pitted dates, chopped
2 tablespoons (¼ stick) butter or margarine
2½ cups Rice Krispies or puffed rice cereal
¾ cup shredded coconut, unsweetened

1. Soften the dates with the butter over medium heat, stirring constantly. Remove from the stove.
2. Mix in the Rice Krispies with a spatula or knife, using a cutting motion.
3. Roll spoonfuls of the date mix into walnut-sized balls.
4. Coat with coconut and set aside to cool.

Crunchies

Yield: 24-30

2 cups old fashioned rolled oats
1 cup flour
½ cup sugar
1 cup shredded coconut, unsweetened

8 tablespoons (1 stick) butter
⅓ cup golden syrup (page 11)
1 teaspoon baking soda

1. Mix the first four ingredients in a mixing bowl.
2. Heat the butter and syrup in a saucepan, while stirring, until the mixture reaches boiling point.
3. Remove from the stove and add the baking soda. Stir briskly as it foams up.
4. Add the syrup mix to the dry ingredients and mix well.
5. Press firmly into a lightly greased baking tray, to a thickness of ¼-½ inch.
6. Bake at 275° F for 20-25 minutes. Do not overbake. Crunchies must be light brown and soft when they come out of the oven.
7. Cut into blocks while warm. Crunchies will harden as they cool.

Old fashioned rolled oats cookies

Yield: 30

1 cup (2 sticks) butter, room temperature
1 cup crunchy brown sugar
1 cup flour
2 cups old fashioned rolled oats

1 cup shredded coconut, unsweetened
1 teaspoon vanilla extract
½ teaspoon baking soda dissolved in 3 tablespoons hot water

1. Cream the butter and sugar in a large mixing bowl, until light and fluffy.
2. Mix in the remaining ingredients.
3. Lightly roll teaspoonfuls of dough between hands and flatten slightly with two fingers before arranging on a greased or lined baking sheet. Allow space for spreading.
4. Bake at 350° F for 13-15 minutes, until lightly browned. Cool slightly before transferring to a cooling rack to crisp.

Custard cookies

Yield: 30-36

2 cups flour
⅔ cup custard powder (page 10)
¾ cup confectioners powder sugar
¼ teaspoon salt
1¼ cups (2½ sticks) butter, room temperature

1. Mix all the dry ingredients in a food processor or large bowl.
2. Blend in the butter or mix with an electric beater until the consistency changes to dough.
3. Knead lightly.
4. Place walnut-sized balls onto a lined or greased baking sheet.
5. Flatten slightly with a fork.
6. Bake at 350° F for 15-18 minutes. Remove the cookies from the oven before they brown, as they must not be overbaked. Cookies will harden as they cool.

Gingernuts

Yield: 48

8 tablespoons (1 stick) butter or margarine
½ cup golden syrup (page 11)
2½ cups flour
1 cup sugar
1 tablespoon ground ginger
1 teaspoon baking soda
pinch of salt
1 egg, whisked

1. Heat the butter and syrup in a saucepan until the butter has melted. Remove from the heat and set aside to cool slightly for a few minutes.
2. Sift the dry ingredients into a mixing bowl.
3. Pour the butter-syrup mixture over the dry ingredients, stir, add the egg and mix well.
4. Roll into walnut-sized balls and flatten slightly with two fingers.
5. Arrange on a lined or greased baking sheet.
6. Bake at 375° F for 10-12 minutes, until lightly browned.

Notes

A little crunchy brown sugar can be sprinkled over the biscuits once they are removed from the oven.

Date muffins

This mixture should stand for a couple of hours or overnight before baking. It can be kept in the refrigerator for up to 5 days and baked as needed.

Yield: 18

2 eggs
⅔ cup brown sugar
½ cup oil
2 cups milk

2 cups multigrain cereal flakes
1 cup whole wheat flour
1 cup white flour
2 teaspoons baking soda
2 teaspoons baking powder
½ teaspoon salt
1 cup dates, pitted and chopped

1. Whisk the first four ingredients together in a large mixing bowl.
2. Add the remaining ingredients and stir until just blended. Do not overmix.
3. Cover and refrigerate for a couple of hours or overnight.
4. Spoon the batter into greased muffin pans, and bake at 350° F for about 20 minutes, until baked through. Serve warm with butter.

Notes

Baked muffins freeze well.

Raisins, cranberries or tart cherries can be used instead of dates, and ½ cup of pecan nuts can be added to the batter for a nutty variation.

Fruit cake

*Dark, rich and moist cake traditionally served at Christmas
and at weddings. It can be served as is, decorated with nuts and
cherries, or frosted. If frosted, it is covered first with a layer of
almond paste and then with royal icing. The frosted cake is then
elaborately decorated with royal icing lace and trellis work, and
topped with sprays of sugar (or fresh) flowers.*

Yield: 1 7½-8 inch round or square cake

Prepare the cake tin before making the cake. Line the tin
with a layer of aluminum foil, shiny side out, and a double
layer of parchment paper. Let the sides stand proud of the
tin so that a foil 'lid' can be used to cover the cake during
baking, to prevent it from becoming too dark.

8 tablespoons (1 stick) butter
⅔ cup dark brown sugar
½ cup orange juice
2 tablespoons marmalade
¾ pound raisins
½ pound sultanas
¼ pound pitted dates, chopped
¼ pound dried cranberries
2 crystallized pineapple rings, cut up

¼ cup brandy
1 teaspoon baking soda
½ cup slivered almonds

2 cups flour
1 tablespoon unsweetened cocoa
1 teaspoon ground allspice
½ teaspoon ground cinnamon
¼ teaspoon ground nutmeg

¼ teaspoon ground ginger
pinch of salt
1 teaspoon baking powder
2 eggs, whisked

brandy or sherry

1. Place the butter, sugar, orange juice, marmalade and all the dried fruit in a large saucepan.
2. While stirring continuously, bring to the boil and simmer until the sugar has dissolved.
3. Remove from the heat and stir in the brandy, baking soda and nuts.
4. Sift all the dry ingredients together and fold them into the fruit mixture, along with the eggs, to form a thick, wet batter. Add a little water if the mixture is too stiff.
5. Make sure that all the ingredients are well combined.
6. Scoop into the prepared cake tin and level the top with a spatula.
7. Bake at 300° F for 1 hour. Cover the cake loosely with foil, shiny side up, and bake for a further 30-60 minutes, until the cake is baked through.
8. Leave the cake in the tin to cool and then turn it out carefully.
9. Sprinkle with a little sherry or brandy before wrapping in greaseproof paper and storing in an airtight container.

Notes

Fruit cake is typically stored for several weeks before serving and is periodically sprinkled with a little brandy or sherry. However, long-term storage may not be advisable in hot, humid areas. Monitor for any signs of mold growth or spoilage.
Fruit cake freezes well.

Raisin bread

Buttermilk rusks

Brown bread

Muesli

Breads, Buns, Rusks & Cereals

White bread

Yield: 2 medium loaves

6 cups white flour
1 tablespoon sugar
2 teaspoons salt
2¼-ounce sachets instant active dry yeast or 1 tablespoon
instant active dry yeast
2 tablespoons olive oil
2¼-2½ cups warm water

1. Combine the flour, sugar, salt and yeast in a large mixing bowl.
2. Add the oil and water and mix very well to form a soft dough. Add a little flour if the dough is too wet to handle, but keep the dough as moist as practically possible.
3. Turn the dough out onto a floured surface and knead thoroughly until the dough is smooth and elastic.
4. Shape the dough into a large ball and return it to the mixing bowl, which can be lightly oiled.
5. Cover the dough with cling wrap or a damp dishcloth and set it aside to rise in a warm place, for 50-60 minutes, until about double its size.
6. Lightly knock down the dough, and divide it between two medium oiled and lightly floured bread tins (9 x 5 x 3 inches).
7. Allow the dough to rise for a further 40-50 minutes, until the volume doubles again.
8. Bake at 400° F for 20 minutes, and then at 350° F for a further 20-30 minutes, until baked through. Remove from the oven and turn out onto a cooling rack.

Notes

Instead of instant active dry yeast, 2¼-ounce sachets of active dry yeast or 1 tablespoon of active dry yeast can be used. Dissolve 1 teaspoon of the sugar in about ½ cup of the warm water. Stir in the yeast and set aside to froth for about 10 minutes. Add to the dry ingredients with the oil and remaining water, while mixing.

When the dough is knocked down, it can be placed into a large, oiled, cast iron pot or Dutch oven instead of the bread pans, to double in size before baking, as above. When prepared in this manner, it is reminiscent of "potbrood" (pot bread), which was buried and baked in a sealed pot, surrounded by hot ash and coals.

Bread dough can be shaped into bread rolls. When the dough is knocked down, form into rolls and set aside to double in size before baking at 350° F for about 20 minutes.

Bread dough can be used to make vetkoek (page 35).

A table model food mixer with a dough hook attachment is ideal for kneading yeast products.

When bread is baked through, it sounds hollow when tapped.

Brown seed loaf

A quick, one-rise stir yeast bread.

Yield: 2 medium loaves

½ cup bulgur, medium or coarse grind
1 cup boiling water
2 cups whole wheat flour
2 cups white flour
1½ teaspoons salt
1 cup rolled oats
1 cup sunflower seeds
2 ¼-ounce sachets instant active dry yeast or 1 tablespoon instant active dry yeast
1 tablespoon honey
⅓ cup oil
2¼-2½ cups warm water

2 tablespoons sesame seeds

1. Place the bulgur and boiling water in a small bowl. Set aside for at least 40 minutes.
2. Mix all the remaining ingredients, excluding the warm water and sesame seeds, in a large mixing bowl.
3. Add the bulgur with any unabsorbed water.
4. Stir in the warm water to form a soft dough. Mix well to combine all the ingredients.
5. Divide between 2 oiled and lightly floured bread tins (9x5x3 inches).
6. Sprinkle sesame seeds over the top.
7. Put the tins in a warm place for 40-60 minutes, until the dough has doubled in size.

8. Bake at 400° F for 20 minutes and then at 350° F for a further 25-30 minutes. Remove from the tins and cool on a cooling rack.

Notes

Cracked wheat can be used instead of bulgur.

Instead of instant active dry yeast, add 2 ¼-ounce sachets of active dry yeast or 1 tablespoon of active dry yeast to a cup containing 1 teaspoon of the honey and about ½ cup of the warm water. Mix and set aside to froth for 10-15 minutes. Add to the ingredients with the bulgur.

Raisin bread

Yield: 1 small loaf

2½ cups flour
1¼ - ounce sachet instant active dry yeast or 2 teaspoons
instant active dry yeast
2 tablespoons sugar
½ teaspoon salt
¾ cup seedless raisins
¼ teaspoon aniseed, optional
3 tablespoons butter
½-¾ cup buttermilk
1 egg

Glaze
1 tablespoon sugar, dissolved in
1½ tablespoons boiling water

1. Combine the flour, yeast, sugar, salt, raisins and aniseed
   in a mixing bowl.
2. Warm the butter with the buttermilk in a small saucepan until the butter melts.
3. Whisk the egg in a jug and add the butter-buttermilk
   mixture to the egg.
4. Mix the liquid ingredients into the dry ingredients to
   form a soft, moist dough. If the dough is too dry, add a
   little more buttermilk or water, and if too wet, a little
   flour.
5. Turn out onto a floured surface and knead until the
   dough is smooth and elastic.

6. Lightly oil the mixing bowl. Form the dough into a ball and return it to the mixing bowl. Cover the dough with cling wrap or a damp dishcloth and set it aside, in a warm place, to rise. After 50-60 minutes, it will have doubled in size.
7. Knock the dough down lightly and divide it into 8 balls. Pack the balls snugly in a greased bread pan (9x5x3 inches).
8. Set the pan aside in a warm place for about 40 minutes, until the dough has doubled in size.
9. Bake at 400° F for 10 minutes, and then lower the temperature to 350° F for a further 30-40 minutes.
10. Turn out onto a cooling rack and glaze the top. Serve warm with butter.

Notes

If active dry yeast is used instead of instant active dry yeast, dissolve 1 teaspoon of the sugar in ¼ cup of warm water. Stir in 1 ¼-ounce sachet of active dry yeast or 2 teaspoons of active dry yeast, and set aside for 10-15 minutes to froth. Add to the dry ingredients with the buttermilk mix.

A table model food mixer with a dough hook attachment is ideal for kneading yeast products.

Hot cross buns

Traditionally eaten at Easter.

Yield: 18

Buns

4 cups flour

2 ¼ -ounce sachets instant active dry yeast or 4 teaspoons instant active dry yeast

¼ cup sugar

1 teaspoon salt

2 teaspoons ground cinnamon

2 teaspoons ground allspice

¼ teaspoon ground cloves

½ teaspoon ground nutmeg

1 ½ cups mixed dried fruit, e.g., raisins, sultanas, cranberries, cherries, blueberries

6 tablespoons (¾ stick) butter or margarine

1 ½ cups buttermilk

2 eggs

Pastry dough for crosses

2 tablespoons (¼ stick) butter

½ cup flour

iced water

Glaze

¼ cup apricot jam

¼ cup sugar

¼ cup water

1. First make the buns. Mix all the dry ingredients, including the fruit, in a large mixing bowl.
2. Warm the butter with the buttermilk in a small saucepan until the butter melts.
3. Whisk the eggs in a jug and add the buttermilk-butter mixture to the egg.
4. While mixing, pour the liquid ingredients over the dry ingredients. The dough must be fairly moist, as the dried fruit will absorb some of the moisture. Add a little more buttermilk or water if necessary. Mix thoroughly.
5. Turn out onto a floured surface and knead the dough until it becomes soft, smooth and elastic. If it is too wet to knead, add a little flour.
6. Lightly oil the mixing bowl. Shape the dough into a ball and place it in the mixing bowl.

7. Cover the dough with cling wrap or a damp dishcloth and set it aside to rise in a warm place for 40-50 minutes, until it has doubled in size.
8. Meanwhile, make the pastry dough for the crosses. Rub the butter into the flour and cut in the water to form a dough.
9. Shape the pastry dough into a ball and refrigerate until needed.
10. Lightly knock down the bun dough and divide it into 18 pieces.
11. Shape the pieces of dough into round buns and flatten slightly.
12. Place the buns on a greased and lightly floured baking tray, fairly close together.
13. Leave the buns to rise in a warm place, until they have again doubled in size. This will take about 30 minutes.
14. Meanwhile, thinly roll out the pastry dough on a lightly floured surface. Cut strips of the desired width and length for the crosses.
15. Just before baking the buns, moisten the strips with cold water and position them to form crosses on top of the buns. The water fuses the pastry to the dough.
16. Bake at 350° F for 20-25 minutes.
17. Prepare the glaze. Heat the jam, sugar and water together in a small saucepan, stirring until the sugar dissolves.
18. Boil for a few minutes until the syrup thickens.
19. Glaze the buns with the syrup as soon as they are removed from the oven. Serve warm with butter.

Notes

If active dry yeast is used instead of the instant active dry yeast, dissolve 1 teaspoon of the sugar in ½ cup of warm water. Stir in 2 ¼-ounce sachets of active dry yeast or 4 teaspoons of active dry yeast and set aside for 10-15 minutes to froth. Add to the dry ingredients, together with the buttermilk and egg mixture.

A table model food mixer with a dough hook is ideal for kneading yeast products.

Buttermilk rusks

Biscotti-like cookies traditionally served with the first cup of tea or coffee of the day. Typically dunked in a warm drink before eating.

Yield: about 60

7 cups flour
3½ tablespoons baking powder
2 teaspoons salt
⅔ cup sugar
1 cup (2 sticks) butter, room temperature
2 eggs
1½ cups buttermilk

1. Mix the flour, baking powder, salt and sugar in a large mixing bowl and rub in the butter.
2. Whisk the eggs and buttermilk in a jug until well blended.
3. Add the buttermilk mixture to the flour mixture and mix to form a pliable dough. Knead very well. Add a little buttermilk or water if the dough is too dry.
4. Break off pieces of dough and roll into golf ball-sized balls.
5. Pack the balls of dough together snugly in a deep baking tin or bread pans, which have been oiled and lightly floured.
6. Bake at 400° F for 20 minutes. Lower the temperature to 350° F and bake for a further 30-40 minutes, until done.
7. Tip out of the pan(s) and break into pieces, using two forks.
8. Dry at 200° F for 3-4 hours, or overnight in a warming drawer.
9. When quite cool, pack the rusks into airtight containers and store in a cool, dry place.

Muesli

Yield: 3 pounds, approximately

2 pounds old fashioned rolled oats
1 cup mixed nuts, e.g., walnuts, pecans, hazelnuts, almonds,
cashews
1 cup sunflower and/or pumpkin seeds
¼ cup sesame seeds or flaxseed
½ cup shredded coconut, unsweetened

¼ cup honey
¼ cup oil
1 tablespoon coconut oil

1 cup mixed dried fruit, e.g., raisins, cranberries, apricots,
figs, mango, cherries
ground cinnamon
ground ginger

1. Mix the first five dry ingredients in a large, ovenproof
    dish.
2. Microwave the honey and oils in a measuring jug for
    25-30 seconds.
3. Pour the liquid ingredients over the dry ingredients and
    mix thoroughly.
4. Bake at 325° F for 35 minutes, mixing after about 20
    minutes.
5. Remove from the oven and add the fruit with a sprin-
    kling of cinnamon and/or ginger.
6. Mix well and set aside to cool before packing into an
    airtight container.

Notes
The ratio of ingredients can be adjusted according to avail-
ability and taste preferences.

Granola

Yield: 1 pound, approximately

2 cups old fashioned rolled oats
¾ cup whole wheat flour
2 cups Weetabix whole grain biscuits, crushed
¾ cup multi-grain flakes
1 cup sunflower seeds
1 cup mixed nuts, e.g., sliced/slivered almonds, walnut- and pecan-pieces
¼ cup sesame seeds

½ cup oil
½ cup honey
1 teaspoon vanilla extract

1. Combine the dry ingredients in a large bowl.
2. Whisk the oil, honey and vanilla in a measuring jug. Microwave for 30 seconds and add them to the dry ingredients.
3. Mix well and spread out onto one or two baking trays.
4. Bake at 275° F for 30-40 minutes.
5. Remove from the oven, crumble and return to the oven (switched off). The granola will harden as it cools. When cold, pack into container(s).

Dried fruit chutney

Apricot fruit rolls

Brown cow

Fruit mince meat

Dom Pedro

Preserves & Beverages

Dried fruit chutney

Spicy condiment for meats.

Yield: 4-5 pints

½ pound dried apricots
½ pound dried peaches
½ pound seedless raisins
3 cups boiling water
3 large cloves garlic, chopped
2 onions, chopped
1 teaspoon salt
1¾ cup dark brown sugar

1½ teaspoons ground coriander
¾ teaspoon ground ginger
½ teaspoon cayenne pepper, optional
2 cups cider vinegar
3 cups brown malt vinegar (e.g., Old English Fish & Chip Vinegar)

1. Dice or coarsely mince the apricots, peaches, and raisins.
2. Place in a large, heavy-based saucepan. Add the water, cover with a lid and set aside overnight, or heat to boiling point and boil for 5 minutes. Remove from the heat.
3. Add all the remaining ingredients to the soaked or boiled fruit. Mix well and bring to the boil, while stirring, to dissolve the sugar.
4. Lower the temperature slightly, but keep the chutney at a rolling boil (bubbling faster than when simmering). Do not cover with a lid.
5. The longer it boils, the thicker the chutney will become. The color will darken slightly.
6. Stir occasionally and lower the heat if necessary, to prevent the chutney from burning.
7. After 45-60 minutes the chutney will have the consistency of jam.
8. Decant the chutney into suitable hot, sterilized bottles or jars and seal.
9. Allow the flavors to blend for a couple of weeks before using.

Fruit mince meat

A spicy fruit filling for Christmas mince pies.

Yield: 2½ pounds, approximately

¾ cup (1½ sticks) butter
1 cup dark brown sugar
¼ cup cider vinegar
3-4 cooking apples, e.g.,
Granny Smith, peeled and
diced, approximately 4 cups
¼ cup lemon juice
½ teaspoon lemon zest
1 cup seedless raisins
½ cup dried cranberries
½ cup sultanas or golden
raisins
½ cup dried tart cherries
½ cup marmalade
1 tablespoon ground allspice
1 teaspoon ground ginger
½ teaspoon ground nutmeg
¾ teaspoon salt
3 tablespoons brandy

1. Heat the butter and sugar in a large, heavy-based sauce-pan and stir until the butter has melted and the sugar has dissolved.
2. Add all the remaining ingredients and mix well.
3. Heat to boiling point, while stirring.
4. Lower the heat and simmer, uncovered, for 30 minutes, stirring occasionally.
5. Spoon into suitable hot, sterilized jars and seal.

Notes

Fruit mince was originally made with minced meat, suet, apples, dried fruit, brandy and cider. Today the meat is omitted and, in some cases, the suet.

Instead of the butter, 4 ounces of diced suet can be used. The mixture should then simmer for 1½ hours.

Crystallized orange peel

Yield: 10 ounces, approximately

4 oranges
2 cups sugar
water

1. Remove the peel of each orange in four segments.
2. Place the peel in a saucepan, cover it with water and bring to the boil.
3. Boil until the peel is very soft, 1-1½ hours, replenishing water as necessary.
4. Drain and cut the peel into thin strips with a pair of kitchen shears.
5. Make the syrup by combining the sugar with 1 cup of water in a saucepan. Heat to boiling point while stirring, so that the sugar is dissolved by the time it starts to boil.
6. Boil without stirring for about 20 minutes, until the syrup reaches the soft-ball stage (238° F).
7. Add the peel and simmer for about 30 minutes, until most of the syrup has been absorbed.
8. Drain well and roll in sugar before storing in an airtight container.

Notes

Instead of rolling the citrus peel in sugar, it can be dipped in melted chocolate using a pair of tweezers.

Apricot fruit rolls

apricots
sugar

1. Wash, stone and mince the apricots or use a food processor to chop them up finely.
2. Measure the fruit pulp, in cups, to determine the amount of sugar needed. The rule of thumb is that 1 cup of sugar is added for every 1 cup of fruit pulp. The quantity of sugar added will, however, depend on the sweetness of the fruit. If the apricots are very sweet, start by adding 2 tablespoons of sugar for every cup of fruit pulp.
3. Add the sugar, mix well and taste. Add more sugar if necessary.
4. Line baking trays with parchment paper and grease well with butter.
5. Spread a thin layer of the fruit mixture evenly over the paper.
6. Dry in the sun for 12 hours in a sheltered area free of flies, birds and ants.
   OR
   Dry in an evaporator, as per directions.
   OR
   Bake in the oven, on convection, at 170° F for about 3 hours.
7. When the fruit is dry, remove the fruit sheet from the paper, sprinkle it with sugar and roll it up tightly.
8. Cut off any brittle edges and cut the fruit roll into convenient lengths. Store in an airtight container in a cool place.

Notes
Nectarines, pears, guavas, mangos and figs are suitable fruits for making fruit rolls.

Lemon syrup

Yield: about 2½ cups syrup

2 cups lemon juice
zest of two lemons
1½-2 cups sugar
¼ teaspoon salt

1. Heat the ingredients together in a saucepan, while stirring continuously, until the sugar dissolves. Do not boil.
2. Strain, bottle and refrigerate.
3. Serve diluted with water or soda water and crushed ice.

Brown cow

Combine Coca-Cola with milk in a glass, at a ratio of 2:1.

White cow

Combine ginger beer with milk in a glass, at a ratio of 2:1.

Orange-guava cocktail

Combine orange juice with guava juice in a glass, at a ratio of 1:1.

Fruit punch

Yield: about 4 pints

4 cups apricot juice, refrigerated
1 30-ounce can fruit cocktail in natural fruit juice, refrigerated
passion fruit pulp, optional
2 cups ginger beer, refrigerated
soda water, refrigerated, to taste
crushed ice

1. Combine the apricot juice, fruit cocktail (with its juice) and passion fruit pulp in a punch bowl.
2. Add the ginger beer, soda water and ice just before serving.

Notes
For an alcoholic punch, add dry white wine or vodka to taste.

Dom Pedro

An after-dinner milkshake with a bit of a kick.

2 servings

1 cup full cream vanilla ice cream
½ cup Amarula cream (page 10) or Bailey's Irish cream, well chilled
¼ cup heavy cream, whipped

1. Blend or whip the ice cream in a blender or bowl until soft and smooth.
2. Add the remaining ingredients and blend or mix well.
3. Pour into two chilled glasses and serve with straws.

Iced coffee

A rich, coffee-flavored milkshake.

2 servings

¼ cup very strong black coffee or
4 teaspoons instant coffee powder mixed with
1 tablespoon boiling water
2 cups full cream vanilla ice cream
¾ cup milk
¼ cup heavy cream, whipped

cocoa powder

1. Chill the coffee in the freezer for about 10 minutes.
2. Beat or blend the ice cream, milk and coffee together until thick and smooth.
3. Fold in ⅔ of the whipped cream.
4. Pour into two attractive glasses and decorate with the remaining cream and a sprinkling of cocoa powder. Serve immediately, with a straw.

Iced rooibos tea

Refreshing health drink. Red bush tea, a flowering shrub that is unique to the Cederberg region of South Africa, has a distinctive flavor and is renowned for its health and beauty benefits.

4-5 rooibos (red bush) tea bags
1 cup boiling water
sugar or honey to taste
cold water
ice cubes

1. Combine the tea bags and boiling water in a heat-proof jug (e.g., Pyrex measuring jug). Set aside to steep and cool down.
2. When cool, pour the concentrate into an attractive jug with two to three cups of cold water. Sweeten to taste and top up with crushed ice.
3. Garnish with lemon wedges and fresh mint leaves.

A

B

P

Q